Newer 911 and an instant classic: 911 GTRS 4.0 with aerodynamic aids front and rear.

Introduction

Porsche's drive to perfection has its roots in a design and engineering ethos that has become personified by a car: the 911 or 'Nine Eleven'. Iconic is an overused word, but in the case of the Porsche 911, it *is* a valid definition. This car has straddled the world sports-car stage for five decades: across all its incarnations 911 has defined what Porsche means and even stepped into the realm of the supercar and motor sport legend. Indeed, even the numbers on the badge '911' have become iconic. This is a car about design and driving. You may think many cars are, but not all achieve such status, and few approach the 911 for its character, appeal and longevity.

In its current model range, 911 is a larger car than its early ancestors, yet it remains probably the most desired sports car in the marketplace. Some purists may feel that it has lost a bit of its original ethos, but others might say it has simply evolved and moved with the times.

The Porsche brand is globally renowned and has become a marketing tool beyond even its cars. Yet surely it is the cars that should define the brand – 911 still does – but we might suggest that so too does the Porsche Cayman GT4. And you cannot ignore where it all started, the essential Porsche 356, without which Porsche and its 911 design language would not exist today.

Despite a couple of 'moments' en route, the 911's is an amazing story, one of pure engineering and design genius stemming from the foundations of Porsche itself – set by the guiding hand of its famous father, Ferdinand Porsche (1875–1951).

In contrast to current perceptions of Porsche as an elite or upmarket German brand of expensive taste, Ferdinand Porsche was not German by birth nor a member of the upper class – quite the opposite in fact. The metamorphosis of Porsche's car company (which once also built tractors) into today's millionaire's brand of preference was a long journey and was ignited by the Porsche 356 and then defined by the 911.

Of 924, 944, 968 and 928? Well, that's another story – one of great interest – but it's not the 911 story. Some think that the 356 and then the 911 have Volkswagen (VW) ancestry, yet this is not wholly accurate. True, the first Porsche production car did share some ideas and many parts with the (Porsche-designed) VW Type 1 'Beetle', but the truth is that by the time Porsche had turned its VW-engined 356 prototype into the mass-production 356, the VW-derived engine of that car had been reworked. Soon afterwards, a fundamentally new Porsche engine was designed. The point is that Porsche himself designed the VW components that later appeared in the 356, the car that people say is VW-derived.

Because the Beetle was rear-engined, and so too were the Porsche 356 and 911, some observers made a link between them, but failed to observe that most Fiats, Renaults, Simcas, Skodas and many other cars of the 1950s were rear-engined too. Even Mercedes-Benz had built a rear-engined production car in the 1930s and the British Rover Company designed one in 1930. The British also persevered with rear-engined cars into the late 1960s in the form of the Hillman Imp – despite the Mini's success. Some Japanese cars were also rear-engined. Mr DeLorean's device was rear-engined, too. Today the smallest new Renault and the Smart car also retain the rear-engined configuration.

Top: Classic 'small bumper' 912 (of 1966 build): spot lamps, Fuchs wheels and racing specification at Prescott Hill Climb. Who said 912s couldn't mix it? Being lighter, they were nimble if less powerful than a flat-six 911.

Above: Perfect rears: a range of early-era 911s in classic colours – two 911S 2.4 litres and an earlier blue car, all courtesy of Autofarm, the Porsche perfectionists.

So there have been a few misconceptions about rear engines and so-called VW and Porsche cars along the way, just as there have been about the Porsche family and the Nazi dictatorship under which they lived, worked and took their orders from during the Second World War.

But above all, there lies project 901, the car that became the 911. The 911 was all new: everything from the wheels up was of Porsche design. Is this why 911 *is* Porsche? From Ferdinand Porsche's son and grandson, 'Ferry' Porsche and 'Butzi' Porsche respectively, from Porsche family member Ferdinand Piëch, to Komenda, Fuhrmann, Bott, Mezger, Lapine, Laagij, Mobius, Mueller, Soderberg and so many others, of the small team that created the original, and its 50-plus-year reign as the queen of the sports coupés, the tale of the 911 to date *is* Porsche. The shape, the feel, the sound – that flat-six symphony – all are part of the 911's mystique. Then there is the driving experience, which is also unique and more akin to piloting a fighter aircraft than lounging in a GT (grand tourer) car.

The 911 has undergone several distinct chapters: 1964 to 1977 saw the first incarnation of the 'pure' 911; then its development via the 'RS' ('Rennsport' or motor racing) series into a larger-engined machine before a turbocharged '930' series. From 1978 to 1989 came its mid-life when the original underpinnings were further modified, yet the essential, original car lay underneath. After 1989 came the 964 series and major engineering revisions to structure, engine, parts, interiors and technology. Then came the further-developed and restyled 993-series era of 1993 to 1997, before major modernization and rationalization gave us the 1998 debut of the water-cooled 996 series that also consisted of a departure from the evolved styling that had not really changed in over three decades.

In the current era, 2004 to date, we have seen a return to a clearer 911 ethos within a modernized chassis and engine across the 997–991 series and variants beyond. And of course, electric power beckons as turbocharging fades.

911 has not been without its issues in engineering and ownership, but the owners' enthusiasm has endured and Porsche have done what they have always done: evolved, refined and perfected their 'Porscheism'. Porsche owners' clubs thrive all over the world. (Porsche Club GB owners' cars and experiences feature in this book.)

Here in this second title in the CarCraft series, the 911 story is told through the focus of engineering, design and through commentary upon its modelling: Porsche has always supported car models and still sells a stunning range of them alongside its full-scale cars in its dealerships. Model manufacturers have always loved the 911 and so have modellers.

This book is a new take on an old story, mirroring the 911's own such tale.

Origins: Icon of Driving & Design

German engineering has a significant place in the history of the motor car and it also occupies notable ground in aerospace and science. However, German technology's reputation was tainted by its role in the Second World War. But German (not Nazi) engineering was, before 1933 and after 1945, of global importance and remains so today.

One of the greatest names of the first great age of the motor car, 1900–30, and of today's automotive era, is that of Porsche, the company founded by Ferdinand A. Porsche. Porsche, the company, is revered the world over for its engineering and rightly so. Porsche makes many cars, not just the 911 range, but it is the 911 that frames this southern German corporate and engineering legend. Porsche, the man and the company, were in fact originally Austrian and born amid the changing map of Europe when the old territories of Bohemia, Silesia and an Austro-Hungarian empire morphed into what today we recognize as Germany, Poland, Austria, the Czech Republic and Slovakia, but was then in the eye of a central European enclave of car and aviation design that exploded onto the world stage from about 1900 onwards.

Bohemia gave us engineering-related things including some of the great names of car design and automotive engineering: Austro-Daimler, Laurent and Klemin, Lohner, N.S.U., Praga, Rumpler, Skoda, Steyr, Tatra, to name just some. Hans Ledwinka was perhaps the leading Bohemian automobile engineer/designer prior to the ascendency of F. A. Porsche.

Into this realm of central European engineering was born Ferdinand Porsche in 1875 in Maffersdorf, North Bohemia

Top: This lovely blue 356 Cabriolet captures the essence of early Porscheism.

Above: The essential 356 ellipsoid sculpture.

The big-like back of a 356 1500, sans bumpers in racing specification.

Above: Perfection of form in the small sports coupé.

Below: 356 remains an icon and a popular classic daily driver.

(today in the Czech Republic). Current perception has it that the global star that is the Porsche brand is German and technically this is legally accurate because Porsche A.G. *is* a Stuttgart-Zuffenhausen-based company. But despite the aura of German engineering, so heavily emphasized, Porsche, the company and its founder Ferdinand Porsche, and nearly all the main engineers and designers were *not* German but Austro-Hungarian.

Ferdinand Porsche's father, Anton, was a tinsmith. His son soon became interested in metalwork, electrics and new technology before being sent to the Vienna Technical College. Aged just 18, Ferdinand was offered a job as an engineering intern at the Bela Egger Company (which became the massive Brown Boveri engineering concern).

By his early twenties, Porsche was running the Bela Egger Company's test laboratory but he would soon join the Jacob Lohner & Co. in Vienna where he went on to design the very early electric cars. Prior to 1899, Porsche's electric cars featured electric motors at each wheel and a clever drive system

By 1900 Porsche had designed, built and raced his first electric car and set a new record with it. It was a car with an aerodynamically faired front. He built a second electric car, for a Mr E. W. Hart of England and, by 1902, had built the Lohner-Porsche 'mixed drive' racing car, soon followed by another variant, the 'Chaise', that had the world's first true, working front-wheel-drive configuration – Cugnot's earlier steam-powered front-drive vehicle aside – and one driven by electric hub-motors: this was the *Radnabenmotor*, an idea which Ferdinand conceptualized in 1899.

By the age of 30, Porsche had joined the famous marque of Austrian-Daimler (latterly Austro-Daimler) in Vienna. There lay the biggest carmaking factory in all of Europe run by Paul Daimler, son of Gottlieb Daimler of Stuttgart. This was

356 in silver with blue stripes and polished hubcaps signals its defining form.

where the German connection was cast and the moment when Porsche became a rising star in the first great age of the motor car.

As early as 1908 Austro-Daimler were working on an aero-engine for use in airships and by 1910 the first aircraft engine in Austria had been created by Porsche. The British licence-built Austro-Daimler aero-engines were designed by Porsche. Being water-cooled, in-line and single block with overhead valves (OHV) were some of the key design features. The *Luftgekühlt* (air-cooled) concept was setting in Ferdinand's mind and in 1912 he created his first air-cooled aero-engine. The Porsche OHV almost-flat-four was revolutionary and Porsche cars would of course latterly champion the air-cooled 'flat'- or 'boxer'-type engine design. VW would also get in on the act.

By the time of the First World War (1914–18), Porsche was creating gun carriages, powered 'mixed-drive' vehicles and trains with hub-motors to ensure lightness via the removal of the need for a heavy locomotive and other devices, for the Austrian military. He also drew up a horizontally opposed engine that was almost a flat type but had its cylinders lying at an angle, in a curious X layout.

Cars for competition were also an Austro-Daimler product line and Porsche created an early lightweight, sporty *voiturette* type – the *Sascha* – in 1922 with an 1,100cc engine. In the *Sascha*, the racer Alfred Neubauer attained 83mph. Later on Ferdinand designed the large and powerful ADM-R model.

In 1923, Ferdinand left Austro-Daimler for employment at Daimler in Stuttgart, Germany, which remains the home of Porsche A.G. to this day. He immediately designed a racing car that won the 1924 Targa Florio endurance race.

Porsche Design
Porsche's fame grew during the 1920s and he decided to start his own design bureau in 1930. The Porsche design office was established at Kronenstrasse 14 in Stuttgart. The company was called Dr.Ing. h.c. Ferdinand Porsche GmbH (Konstrucktionsburo fur Motoren-Fahrzeug, Luftfahrzeug un Wasserfahrzeugbau) or Porsche Construction Office for Motor Vehicles, Aircraft and Water Vehicles.

In this name, Porsche referred to himself as an aviation (*Luft*) and boat/ship (*Wasser*) vehicle engineering expert. Karl Rabe joined him from his role at Austro-Daimler, one that Porsche had helped him achieve. Erwin Komenda, the body designer, also joined the group which included ten other engineers and fabricators. Porsche then hired Josef Mickl (an aviation and flying boat engineer) as an aerodynamicist, as well as several Austrian-trained engineers, all ex-Vienna men including Reimspiess, Froehlich, Kales, Klauser and Zahradnik.

Porsche designed a 1,500cc fastback, two-door, small car for the Neckarsulmer Stricken Union (NSU) in 1933, and we might say that the latter VW Beetle 'copied' its design. Porsche motivated the 1934 Auto Union speed-record car that nudged 200mph, and also influenced a 750kg lightweight Auto Union grand prix car with sixteen cylinders. He also engineered cars for Zundapp, and for the Wanderer Company.

Funding for the Porsche company came in part from no less a figure than the racing proponent A. Rosenberger, until he emigrated to America just before the Nazis came to power in 1933. Adolf Hitler then ordered Porsche to design a Volkswagen *Kleinwagen* (People's Car small car) for the nation's levy-funded *Kraft durch Freude* (Strength through Joy, the large

6   PORSCHE 911: CLASSIC GERMAN SPORTS CAR

Right: Even Porsche's first dashboard was an act of exquisite design and remains so today.

Below: Single vent seen on 356 Speedster rear lid.

state-operated leisure organization that was part of the German Labour Front). The result was the KdF-Wagen which became the ubiquitous Volkswagen 'Beetle' of the mid- to late twentieth century that sold massively worldwide despite its 'Nazi' origins.

In 1934 Hitler called Porsche in and made him consultant to this project under what would become the VW KdF umbrella. Therein lay the seed of controversy, but Porsche never adopted Nazi ideology, having demonstrated concerns over German workers' rights and conditions after seeing how well Ford treated its workers in Detroit. Porsche was never political, never active in the NSDAP – the 'Nazi' party. Like many people in post-1933 Germany, Porsche simply did what he was told. Those who refused, like Hugo Junkers, the aviation pioneer, saw their life's work confiscated (Junkers was dead soon afterwards).

We should briefly note that after the war no charges were brought against Ferdinand Porsche by the Allied powers. Indeed, he was given an official document clearing him of any complicity in war crimes and issued paperwork stating that no charges were to be brought against him; he was a free man. Yet soon afterwards, he would be arrested by the French on spurious political grounds, only then to be freed after having 'advised' Renault engineers on their designs for a new French 'people's car'.

America got to the moon off the back of Nazi weapons of mass destruction and the world entered the swept-wing jet age in military and civil aviation via German and then Nazi-funded wartime research that was rounded up post-May 1945 and shipped off to the victors, Operation *Paperclip* being the headline to that exercise. Swept wings, supersonics and advanced science – much of it of German origin – was rebranded. Engines, transmissions and vehicular technology were also rounded up.

The science of road vehicle aerodynamics, today so fashionable, might arguably be said to have begun with German studies in the 1920s and the University of Stuttgart's pre-war research department. Ferdinand

Porsche invoked aerodynamics in his designs from his very early, pre-1920 days.

Porsche designed the VW Type 1 – the Beetle – in Germany at the orders of the Hitler government but that did not make him a Nazi. The VW Beetle and the VW camper and minibus mobilized much of America and Europe into the 1970s, as owned and driven by people of all creeds, colours and religious persuasions who were happy to ignore such origins.

Significantly, just prior to 1939 Porsche had clothed one of his VW KdF-type air-cooled, mid-rear-engined, swing-axled chassis/floorpans in an amazing sculpted, aerodynamic low-drag body shell and created a sports-racer-type variant. It then evolved into a 'special', as the Type 64, for competition in the 1939 Berlin–Rome rally. The rally was cancelled as war clouds gathered, but in the design of this car, we can see many clues to what was to come after the end of the Second World War.

356

Having moved to Gmund in Austria, Porsche, his son and his small team of engineers were by 1947 producing a diesel-engined Porsche tractor of Type 313 and, of note, creating a new racing car for the Cisitalia Company in Turin. But Porsche had something else in mind: an amalgam of his small family car, the VW KdF Beetle, and the 1939 Type 64 teardrop, low-drag racer he had created. What about blending both into a small but sporty car?

'A sports car for the many' was Ferdinand's suggestion. By August 1947 work on the car that was to define the new Porsche brand, the 356 – the 356th design project of Porsche – began. Weakened by ill health Ferdinand would be dead by 30 January 1951, but the Porsche car legend *had* started. The new car was to be the first, true, mass-produced Porsche-named car and one that founded the ethos of engineering excellence that we know today.

356 as a prototype was initially framed by a one-off and, notably, mid-engined, open-topped, two-seat, alloy-bodied, lightweight sportster that used many VW parts and a VW engine. By the time it became the rear-engined and defining 356 model, it contained far fewer proprietary VW parts. Porsche-designed cylinder heads adorned the VW engine of the 1950 356; in 1952 the engine had major internal components redesigned to Porsche parts; by 1956 it would soon contain an all-Porsche engine created by Fuhrmann. Beyond 1957, there was nothing of VW left in Porsche's engines and little in the suspension or drivetrains. 356 in mass production *was* a true Porsche.

A fixed-head coupé style was chosen with a sleek teardrop cabin turret and roofline. Ellipsoid shapes and rear side windows added to the curved, sculpted look. There were no channels, ridges, stick-on spoilers or flanges; the whole thing was like a pebble smoothed off by water.

The 356's engines ranged from 1 0 litre, 1.1 litre, through to 1.5 litre and 1.6 litre; by the 1960s a 2.0-litre model range was implemented that saw 356 go from austere two-seater to luxury GT sports car known as the 356 C/SC and Carrera model ranges.

356 had gone through a model development life cycle as the 'Pre-A', the A series, B series and the C series. At each stage design and engineering developments took Porsche towards its next stage of existence. The 356A of the mid-1950s still looked like a 356, but underneath it had been recast, with many body and drivetrain engineering changes. Dr-Ing Ernst Fuhrmann was the man behind the development of Porsche's own new engine for the 356 and its ultimate incarnation as the Carrera/GT. Expensive alloy castings and fittings created a high-quality engine that was not cheap to manufacture. Here was laid down the Porsche hallmark of quality.

There was also the famous 356 that was the raw-specification, soft-top 'Speedster' and a folding-roofed 'Cabriolet'. The 356 also begat the 550 series of two-seat, open-cabin, ultra-lightweight, road-legal and circuit-specification racers, and the racing car ultimately framed in public perception by the death of James Dean in his Porsche 550-based Spyder, not a 356 Speedster as some say.

The 550 originally weighed 550kg – hence its nametag. The car was effectively a next-stage development from the genus of the 356 Roadster/Speedster in race trim. From 550 came 550A, and the 718 and RSK variants.

By 1962, the 356 had come of age and entered the elite market of the well-heeled. The 356 1600, the Speedster, the 356GT and the 356 Carrera 2/2000GS became the defining examples of the model's wider production history.

The 356 (with nearly 75,000 examples sold) was a radical departure, not just in terms of design but also in terms of driving. It delivered new standards of performance and handling, a unique 1950s sporting 'drive' yet one which was neither V8-powered nor a collection of 1930s parts and engines rejigged for post-war austerity. 356 was stylish, sporty and like a shiny jewel: such qualities made it popular in America and via Max Hoffman – Porsche's original concessionaire in the US – it carved a brand niche.

Above all, the shape of the 356 – teardrop, low-slung and of pure coupé form – triggered a new post-war design language and set the course of Porsche design in the next car that the company was to produce: the 911 that would take the Porsche brand onto a new global plain of perception.

Design by Detail

Above: 911 originals in race trim at Goodwood over fifty years after 911's launch.

Below: Porsche Blue – early 911 – pure, simple and timeless; note the scale and stance of the car amid its design language.

By 1964 Porsche the car maker was high profile, successful and suddenly the choice of the rich, the famous and the keen driver. The 356, even as a 2.0-litre GT car with luxury trim, was brilliant but ageing, small and still expensive to build and own. Replacing it was one thing, bettering it was the next task. A new car, a completely new car, *not* an update or reiteration (as 356C had been), was surely required.

Enter Project 901. 901 was 911, but French car maker Peugeot owned the rights to the zero or '0' series trademark, so 901 had to become 911.

We can divide the 911 story into three eras or periods that encompass the 1960s, 1980s and beyond the millennium to date. Here in this narrative, we examine the key models in this lineage.

As early as 1957, the small Porsche engineering team began to lay down plans for their new sports car. By 1960 they knew it would be bigger – with two small 'occasional' rear seats and a six-cylinder engine – and it would have improved suspension and handling, all clothed in a stylish new body. But they would search for a style, an acceptable new design, for some time. They knew it had to be beyond quickly dating fashion, to be something timeless. This car required design by detail, a forensic design research thinking that was to become the essence of the 911.

The car would however be rear-engined – truly rear-engined – and this would require much work on the suspension set-up to try and reduce (but not cure) the potentially wayward nature of the rear-biased configuration. The engine would be a 2.0 litre (1,991cc) of at least 130bhp and the body shell would need to be aerodynamically efficient to make the most of the available power. The gear change, steering and controls would also need to meet or exceed the direct and superb behaviours such as found in the 356.

Of note, 911 kept the same type of floor-mounted pedals, the informative steering and the incredible accuracy and fluidity of driving that made the 356 so important on the world stage. 911 was to be no boulevardier, no luxury coupé; instead it would be a proper sports car that might be GT but not one for the lazy driver.

Body

Widely accepted as the work of a young designer who happened to be a member of the Porsche family – Ferdinand's grandson known as 'Butzi' – the 911 also contained design elements from the in-house Porsche team. Erwin Komenda engineered the body into production reality and there was a later debate about the suggestion of his having made a 'tutor's contribution' to Butzi's chosen styling shape – or not. Whatever the questions, 911 was deemed to be penned by a Porsche. Of note it continued the ellipsoid, teardrop form of the 356 but into a modern context.

Of interest was the elegant tail, the 'emotional' or 'graphical' shape of the front windscreen, and the hallmark sculpting of the front wings, bonnet (hood) and headlamps: here was the new 'face' of Porsche. 911's elliptical rear-side window design became another instantly defining hallmark and the deletion of these rear side windows from the Targa version had a major effect upon its looks.

The car had a low front with an unusual 'dip' of the bonnet between the wings, providing good airflow up the car in the straight-ahead position, but actually creating lift, eddies and drag at a side-angle or cross-wind position; there was little that could be done about this unrealized issue other than fitting a front air dam.

Of real interest was the rear end. The shallow angle to the swept 'fastback' rear

Above: This early car is notable for its rear badging script: 911 ready to race. This is the Richard Meaden/Howard Donald car chassis 302056 seen at Goodwood Members' Day; also driven by Chris Harris at Goodwood in the Aldington Trophy.

Left: Turning under power, the 'face' of the 911 is obvious. 901 of Juan Pablo Orjuela – who also drives a 911 RSR.

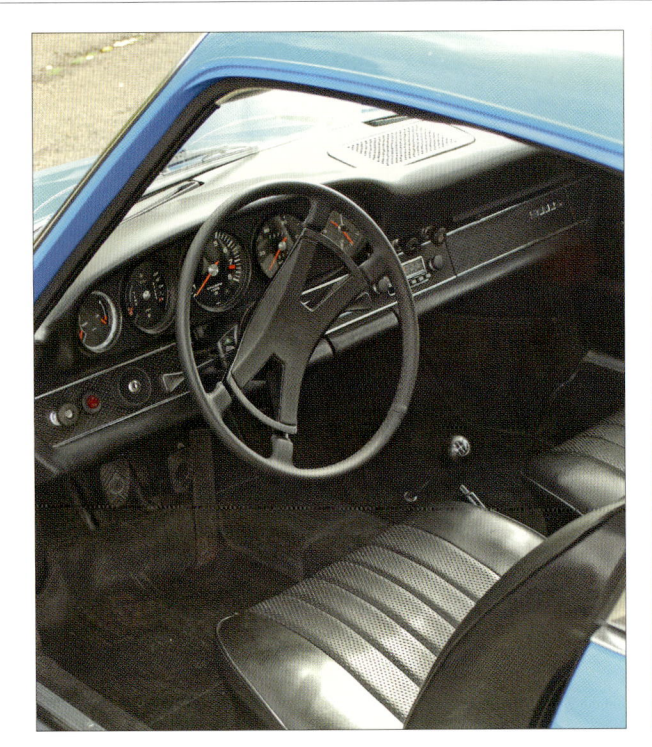

Above left: 911S interior with the revised steering wheel with original-type seats.

Above right: In the background is the famous ducktail rear-deck spoiler to reduce lift and engine venting. In the foreground is a more classic 1970s black-scripted 911 without spoiler.

Right: Black (not chrome) front valance vents were a noteworthy specification change (usually S and T). This gem was a classic Porsche colour. An early car, it has the telltale two-bolt vent mounting – later cars had four per vent.

Bottom: A rarity – one of about forty factory early 1970s development-series cars. Note the handcrafted front and rear wing wheel arch extensions. This car is seen as now modified by Josh Sadler for hill-climb use.

Carrera revived a 356 theme. Side scripts and wheels were available in red, blue or, thanks to British customers' ideas, in black. Carrera RS script in the ducktail says it all.

would normally encourage the designer to try and keep the airflow attached down the rear rump of the car – certainly over and down the rear window and then to a point where the smooth air could be 'triggered' to separate cleanly away off the back of the car. This involves designing-in or fitting a ridge or raised edge or 'spoiler' at the rear, the trailing edge of the car. Such a device can tune the airflow off the car to reduce drag and wake effects, and also reduce aerodynamic lift – the force acting from the smooth, high-speed air flowing down, over and off the back of the car.

But the 911 was rear-engined and had an important need to supply incoming, cooling air to the engine buried in the tail, and to remove or vent-out engine heat, airflow and exhaust from the engine off the already crowded back end of the car.

After much head-scratching and some wind tunnel work on a clay model, the 911 was given a deliberate airflow separation point at the top (not at the bottom) of its rear window. A sharp edge on the roof and a drop down onto the rear windscreen triggered the airflow to separate over the rear windscreen and to reduce its local speed and its 'lift' effect to some degree, although it did not cure the problem.

This design permitted a set, constant airflow behaviour off the roof lip and, vitally, allowed slower-speed air into the engine bay. It also allowed provision for air to vent-out of the car and for the exhaust pipes to be ideally set on the lower rear valance. As the 911 developed into a more powerful car with higher speeds, the issue of aerodynamic lift off its rear became more crucial and various

The rare Carrera script in black on a classic 911.

Still racing: note wing mirror design, ducktail and timing trigger plate mounted to front of car. 911 in the pits.

spoilers – notably the famous ducktail-shaped spoiler (see photos) was fitted to drastically reduce lift for a safer centre of air pressure effect – at the expense of increased drag. Six different rear vent designs were tried for the original 911's engine lid to get the right airflow/heat egress patterns. On subsequent models, there followed the famous 'tea tray' whale tail rear wing or spoiler developments.

Airflow off the back of the 911 was vital in its design and remains so to this day where we see numerous automatically deployed devices to achieve the effect of less lift and more downforce at high speed on new 911 models.

A drag coefficient of C_D 0.381 (corrected) was reliably cited in the Stuttgart University wind tunnel for the early 911 in road-going 'owner' trim including door mirrors and vertical number plate at the front. However, the addition of extra trims, wider wheels and bodywork changes would worsen this figure, not improve it. The cross-sectional frontal area C_DS was a good figure of 0.642. However, wheel arch flares, wider tyres and new trims would make this figure worse. 911's best recorded drag coefficient when fitted with rear spoiler, low drag door mirrors and re-profiling of certain under panels and the front air dam panel was cited at C_D 0.363, which, given its very upright front windscreen angle, is exceptionally good.

Much work would be done to reduce lift over the car's rear deck. The 911's worst (highest) drag coefficient occurred in the G- and H-series 911 when C_D 0.423 was regretfully achieved when the car was fully trimmed but without a front air dam or a rear spoiler. However, the famous 'tea tray' rear spoiler – mounted higher on the rear engine cover (than the ducktail type) and with edge/endplate shaping – reduced lift and drag most beneficially. Such 'tea tray'-louvered and -shaped rear spoiler or wing would last, in developed form, across to the 993 series cars.

Structurally the 911 was all new and incorporated numerous features to increase its rigidity. Strong sills, windscreen A-pillars tied into the firewall, front and rear chassis-type longerons, cross-beams at the bulkhead, and a boxed-in fuel tank (under the front scuttle of the car) all made 911 'safe' but it has to be said that in 1963, knowledge of crash structures and crash testing was in its infancy; 911 was crash-tested of course but it was arguably no more or less safe than other cars. Curiously, the centre B-pillars were seemingly rather thin and not heavily reinforced, whereas the Targa version was fitted with a thick roll-hoop built in at the B-pillar. A collapsible three-piece steering column (with centre pivot section) was fitted as were seatbelts and fire-retardant fittings.

Of interest here is that the early cars were supposed to have black anodized window and trim fittings, but marketers deemed that the look of chrome (or polished stainless steel) looked more expensive. However, across the years, chrome, or black window trim, options have become a key 911 feature: to date you can still opt for extra chrome trim around the side windows on a new 911.

The early 911s had delightful thin front and rear bumpers (some minus a chrome trim strip) and were known as the 'small bumper' cars in later years – not least after the later debut of the 5mph impact-type 'big' bumpers with their obvious external bellows.

911's chassis development engineer Helmuth Bott and lead structures engineer Hans Tomola worked on all aspects of the car's critical ingredients and in under three years, they defined the 911 and its fifty-year future. Prior lead Porsche engineer Karl Rabe had left the company in 1962 and Porsche family member Ferdinand Piëch had joined the engine department as 911's engine was being developed. His later career speaks for itself and needs little description here, suffice to say that 911 is where he started out. By 1966 he was chief development engineer.

Engine

In 1960, many car makers were still producing rear-engined cars, especially sports cars where traction and the related motor sport requirements clearly favoured the rear-engined configuration. 'Father' Porsche's son, 'Ferry', was adamant that Porsche should stick with a rear-engined design and so it did. He also set the short, 87in/2.20m wheelbase: he was insistent that the car remained small and nimble (not something you can say about the recent 911s).

Porsche continued with the small dimensions and low-build of a 'flat', 'boxer' or horizontally opposed engine design. This permitted much easier fitting of a large-capacity six-cylinder engine in the narrow and low confines of the rear of a car. An in-line, upright, tall, heavy V8 or 'straight-six' engine would not fit and would also increase the height of the centre of gravity and adversely affected handling, which was a major issue with the rear-engined layout.

Air-cooling posed few problems for Porsche whose experience of it went back decades. Devoid of a water 'jacket' in a cast 'head' around the engine's mechanicals, the air-cooled engine was lighter and noisier – but what a sound!

The engine design team included project directors Hans Tomola and Klaus von Bucker; design and development men

Classic 911 trio showing specification differences: over riders, strips and chrome work were all regularly revised. The 1970s 2.4-litre cars are often thought to be the best 'original' series 911 variation. The blue car is an early 911S.

Right: Full-fat 911 flat-six 'boxer' engine detail with air filters, and the full installation! That fan was exquisitely engineered (see text).

Below: The 911 rear side window form framed by a red 911 with race-specification front fuel filler in the bonnet/hood panel.

'European' yellow lamps and gunmetal grey paint set off this lovely classic 911 seen at Bicester Heritage.

included Leopold Janstche (an ex-Tatra employee) as leader, with Robert Binder, Host Marchart, Helmutt Rombols, Hans Honick and Helmuth Bott. Ferdinand Piëch led the engine design function and a certain Hans Mezger was vital to the design and would achieve fame for many 911 engine variations.

Having an ex-Tatra engineer (Janstche) on the team may explain why the initial 1960 prototype engine was a pushrod engine with two belt-driven, coaxial cooling fans! This was similar to the last Tatra production engine. But the 911's block would soon develop and dump the pushrod mechanism for overhead cams.

From 1960 to 1964 the engine team crated ten engine development prototypes (some codenamed after birds and insects) and finally settled on an eight (not four) bearing engine with internal lubrication channels through bearings 1 and 8. This was clever stuff. Original 911 engines lacked crankshaft counterweights, but these were latterly added as cubic capacity was increased.

With its defining coaxial, belt-driven 24mm diameter light alloy cooling 'blower' in a jet turbine-type housing as a cooling fan, the issue of cool air around the engine was solved. Only eleven blades needed to be fitted (twenty would have been more normal) and a lightweight plastic shroud funnelled cool air onto the engine banks. Despite its exquisite engineering it actually drained less power off the engine than a standard cooling pump/fan set-up.

With heat exchangers, gearbox, dry-sump-type oiling, exhaust, drivetrain (let alone the later addition of a turbocharger and cooler) and trailing arm suspension forgings, all under the back end, the engine compartment and under tray of the 911 was a busy place. Throw in six, yes, six Solex 'overflow'-type carburettor functions

Design by Detail 15

Above: See at a 911 gathering, this lovely big-bumper car has some interesting specification details. Note unusual wheels.

Centre left: Here we see that later rear spoiler on a standard-bodied rear specification. This rear-spoiler design provided the lowest drag with the best lift-reduction compromise – the trailing lip in rubber was suitably 'sharp' to trim the airflow, something that had not been allowed with the ducktail.

Bottom left: Wonderfully liveried 911 sporting bumper mouldings and a massive 'downforce' rear wing. This car has interesting bodywork modifications.

Bicester Heritage is home to many a 911 gathering: three gems sit and make their design statement.

(no float-chambers) which included a feed pump and a common air duct manifold and things were getting complex. A fuel recovery pump fed fuel back to the main pump; there turned out to be an unexpected problem of flow and mixture that manifested itself in production cars but which had not been seen in testing. By 1967, competition 911s had switched to the Weber carburettor despite every effort from Solex to cure the curious phenomenon.

911 used a hydraulically tensioned, chain-driven, crank-cam mechanism of very high metallurgical quality; cambelts – made of a rubber compound – were too new in 1960 to be totally reliable and Porsche sidestepped this quieter, but less durable option. Hans Mezger and Horst Marchart were the men who developed this vital aspect of the new engine.

Having a Porsche family member on the engine team meant that the usual issue of cost and approval for the spending of it was made easier. Specifying quality and its cost was not a problem.

One benefit of the flat, twin-bank engine was the space for airflow and cooling vanes to dissipate heat – vital without a water-cooling system and engine jacket. The heat loads on the engine were high, so Porsche specified some very expensive-grade aluminium alloys with high nickel content to retain strength as heat effects build-up in the metal.

Built in light alloy with iron-sleeved cylinders with an aluminium case, the engine looked amazing and sounded even better. Zero to 60mph took 8.1 seconds and the top speed nudged 130mph.

The transmission was a five-speed type of an entirely new Porsche design with an unusual finned casing. Full synchromesh was applied to all forward gears. A limited-slip differential would latterly reap huge rewards for drivers, notably in competition. The engine's torque was fed through a single disc clutch and some rather fine gearbox gauges and tolerances which would require later modification as power ratings increased, notably the turbocharger applications.

Suspension

Porsche had owned the design/patent rights to the torsion bar, sprung-tension tube suspension design up until 1950, and applied transverse torsion bars to the 911's rear suspension 'crucible' set-up, which included longitudinal semi-trailing arms and auxiliary springs to the end of the torsion bars travel. Shock absorbers or dampers had pivoted long-travel mounts which aided the ride and handling dynamics that were mounted to stiff points on the body. At the front a very conventional MacPherson-type strut and damper/torsion (not coil) spring units were deployed – notably angled in their mounting, and running through the lower wishbone arms. The 'bump' travel of the suspension was further aided by an extra spring (rubber) set within the mechanism. A transverse tube across the car tied the left and right side suspension dynamics together and added roll-control.

With all these expensive extra suspension design ingredients, there came about the excellent ride and steering response of the 911: notably where the front wheels 'communicated' with the driver via messaging of what was going on up through the steering and the body.

The only real issue was the (throttle) lift-off oversteer, the effect of the rear suspension design under certain dynamic loads and behaviours entering and through a bend. 911 became notorious for this in the hands of a novice driver; a problem exacerbated in the 1970s' 'Turbo' years. The origins of the problem perhaps also lay in the light front of the car (being minus engine), the very short wheelbase and its effect on handling. Narrow tyres didn't help and much work was done to reduce the problem.

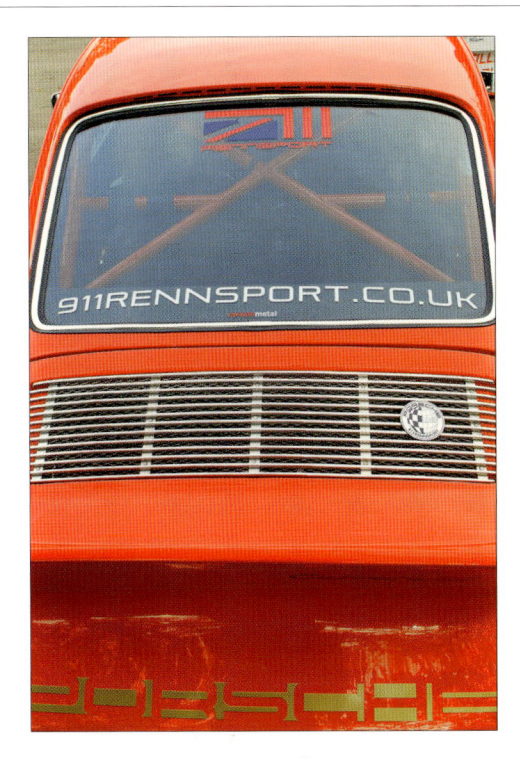

Above left: 'Rennsport' says it all.

Above right: It's that wonderful rear side window shape, fast-back and ducktail detailing that is uniquely 911's design language.

Below right: The later 993 variant had completely revised front and rear panels, Riveria Blue and black window trim framing the sculpture.

The prototype cars had been hand built to forensic tolerances, but suspension settings on the production lines were not quite so accurate and Porsche had to implement special measures to monitor and verify the vital front (and rear) suspension settings to avoid handling problems. Castor, camber, toe-in/-out angles were all vital for correct set-up of this suspension and its resultant effects on handling.

The 'cure' was the very un-Porsche-like quick fix of early 1965: they fitted extra weight into the front of the cars, even those that had been delivered and would come in for a service. Was it lead or cast iron weights? Experts say it was cast iron and 48lb/22kg for two, one fitted into each side of the bumper. Initially weights in bumper over-riders were used but these were mounted near the centre line of the car and had less effect: moving the weights out to the corners of the bumper seemed to help. This aided the balance of the car and its handling, but so too could differing tyre pressures, revised settings or a sack of sand stored in the front luggage hold!

Launch

In 1963, the new engine design had been coded 901 and this was applied to the car's development profile, hence Porsche Type 901.

The first twelve development-build test cars appeared from early 1963 for late-development testing and verification: the first running, fully finished production prototype was numbered chassis # 13.321 as one of twelve such cars. The first full production status 911 'chassis' left the factory line in Stuttgart on 14 September 1964; such cars were built prior to Peugeot leaping to defend their registered '0' name brand. Porsche decided not to argue and came up with '911' by mid-November 1964.

Eighty-two first 'production' 901 vehicles were built from 14 September, but not sold.

Although launched in 1963 at the Frankfurt Motor Show, 911 would not actually go on sale until the latter part of 1964. The open-top, removable-roof section with fixed roll hoop inside the B-pillar would debut as the Targa model in 1966 for the 1967 model year.

911 was beautifully finished and trimmed in a classical sense – nothing flashy, just restrained yet elegant design and engineering. The standard fittings included (highly unusually) electric windscreen-washers with three-speed wipe setting, a laminated windscreen, full instrumentation, a fully padded interior, seatbelt mountings, reclining seats, proper heating and ventilation, and an independent 'winter' cabin heater.

Three things were which took 911 upmarket from 356 were noticeable: the shape of the car, the engine's performance and the equipment. Something else would become noticeable too: the high price and also the issues of high speed and the rear-engine design's dynamic effects via the rear-suspension design.

Technical Specification Porsche Type 901/911: 1964 Model

Body
All-steel monocoque, two-door fastback or aerodynamic design. Targa open-roof version announced 1966, with major tooling changes.
Manufacturer's cited co-efficient of aerodynamic drag: C_D 0.381 (corrected).

Engine
Rear-mounted, six-cylinder 'flat'-type, horizontally opposed.
Air-cooled with aluminium alloy crankcase and cylinders.
Capacity: 1,991cc.
Bore & stroke; 80.0 x 66.0mm.
Single overhead valves.
Compression ratio: 9.0:1 (latterly raised).
Carburation: Solex-type single-choke, then Weber-type triple choke.
Power: 130bhp (DIN) at 6,100rpm.
Max torque: 130lb/ft at 5,200rpm.

Transmission
Rear-wheel drive via manual gearbox. Later 'Sportomatic' semi-automatic option from 1967.

Suspension
Front: independent MacPherson strut with lower wishbones and longitudinal torsion bars.
Rear: independent by trailing arms and transverse torsion bars: telescopic dampers.

Steering
Rack & pinion type.
Brakes: front and rear discs with 11.1in and 11.2in respectively.
Wheels & tyres: steel wheels 4.5in x 15in (5.5in from 1966) 165/HR 15.

Main dimensions
Length: 13ft 8in
Width: 5ft 3.25in
Wheelbase: 7ft 3in (latterly extended)
Height: 4ft 3.5in.
Weight: 20.4cwt/1034kg.

Performance
Max speed: 129.9mph.
0–60mph: 8.5 seconds.

'Big bumpers' with revised mirrors and side details mark this out as a classic mid-life 911 series car.

Variations on a Theme

The early 1964 911s were perhaps the 'pure' representation of a smart but uncomplicated sports car. However, some initial issues were soon obvious and improvement began.

Ventilated disc brakes would also soon be added for 1965. Early 911s used narrow 4.5in-width wheels; by 1966 5.5in wheels had been substituted. Improvements in the engine included new nitrided connecting rods and modified cylinder heads, valves and timing.

The Targa model with its removable roof panel and roll bar hoop was the world's first production version of such a design feature: a 'safety' convertible. As such it was way ahead of the impending US safety legislation for soft-top cars, but caused controversy amongst 911 enthusiasts for its styling variances.

The carburettor problems described (above) would also need solving with a Weber fitment and modifications to mountings and to the air filter. Gear ratios would also be altered with a lower gearing. This meant higher engine revs, but the flat-six could take it – running at just under 7,000rpm flat out did not seem to worry it. This new gearing debuted in the 1966-model-year cars as announced in September 1965.

As early as 1968 the basic 911S was offered with lightweight glass fibre panels and Plexiglas windows for race and rally use. Thin skins, glass fibre and Plexiglas got the weight down to 829kg. A 911 'Monte Carlo' marked the 911's outing at the 1965 rally of that name and was produced for competition use as the start of special series 911s. 1969/70 saw developed, rally-specification 911s being offered for sale from the factory. These cars used thinner metal for some panels, notably the roof. The 911 R 2.0 litre defined the R-series race-specification cars at this time.

A very limited production run of 911 R-type cars was produced for late 1966. Intended for motor sport use, these had lighter body shells (the car weighed under 900kg) and race-tuned engines of 210bhp that could run to 8,000rpm. Four development cars were built under Ferdinand Piëch's lead, and twenty 'production' versions then produced. This was the first 911 to exceed 140mph. With the backing of Piëch and the influential Porsche motor sport leader von Hanstein, the idea was to create a racing series of 911s with 400 examples homologated for the racing regulations. These lightweight 911Rs could have launched the 911 into international motor sport in 1967, but the Porsche company decided not to proceed with the project.

Running parallel to the early series 911s was the 912, the forgotten Porsche and for so long a hidden part of the 911 story.

912

Of particular note, in 1965 Porsche soon realized that its new upmarket 911 was pitched well in excess of the 356's traditional buyers. True, the 356 C series had continued in production to cover 1964's 911 introduction, but it was soon terminated in 1965, leaving Porsche with no direct 'cheap' or standard model line (if ever a Porsche could be called 'standard').

The essential headlamp shape (slightly heavier rimmed on American-specification headlamps) and front wing line simply shout '911'.

A new 911 was over DM5,000 more to buy than a top-of-the-range 356 1600SC.

Enter the 911 body with a four-cylinder engine – at a lower price and a new badge that read 912.

Launched in 1968 to offer previous 356 buyers a base-model 911 choice rather than seeing them shop elsewhere, 912 used a 90bhp flat-four engine that was smaller and lighter than the six-cylinder engine. 912 was a significant 180lb/84kg lighter than a 911 – as if you had got rid of a normal-sized passenger. So although 912 was slower, it handled better because its rear end was lighter, thanks to the smaller engine. Even with a 0–60mph time of over 10 seconds, it was still faster than many contemporary rival sports cars of American, British, French or Italian origin. 912 could just about top 120mph with a following wind and it was otherwise indistinguishable from a 'proper' 911.

Intriguingly, 912's 1.6-litre engine was an old-fashioned pushrod engine development from inside Porsche and of 356 genealogy, but curiously derated by 5bhp to 90bhp. It was fitted with an intake silencer which lowered engine noise. Porsche had to make changes to the tooling for the 912's engine bay at some expense.

Bodies were built by Porsche and by its contractor Karmann; 1966–9 were key years for the 912 and it would see its wheelbase standardized with the 911. 912s bound for the US were encumbered with emissions controls, but the later US market 912E would have a different engine. You could even buy a 912 Targa – today a very rare car.

912 was at launch over £1,000 cheaper than a 911, but on sale in mainland Europe only. But it was soon to reach British roads and then America where it was $3,000 cheaper than a 911. Furthermore it did many more miles to the gallon – touching 32mpg was easy with the five-speed gearbox option.

Just over 31,000 912s were built from 1965 to 1969, with the last cars being a 'second' version as the 1,971cc 912E (injection) big bumper specifically sold in America for the 1975/76 model year only. It could be had with chrome, or black de-chromed window trims and numerous 'sports' options. In fact, from a few feet away it could look like a 911 2.7, until you saw the badge.

912E was an export-only model and of note the engine was different from the first-series 912. Electronically injected, it was based on the engine that had been used in the 914-4 and was thus familiar to American dealers.

For many years the subject of unfair criticism, 912 was the orphan of the 911 story and much maligned. This is a shame and an error because it was a sweet, well-balanced car with good handling and typical Porsche feel. Today, 912s are more appreciated and rising in value.

Above and right: The 911 Targa with black roll-hoop specification and a classic metallic gold finish set off by the funky 1980s seat trim pattern. Very Porsche-design!

Porsche Performance in the 1970s
911 was continuously developed as the 1970s dawned. Refinements to the engine, drivetrain, suspension, trims and specifications took place every summer for the forthcoming model-year announcements usually made in September.

After the 911's launch, it saw the model range consist of 911, then the 911L (130bhp), the 911S (uprated 160bhp engine) and in 1967 the T (Touring) 110bhp model debuted. The 911L had superseded the 'stock' launch 911 model and had improved interior trim and enhanced fittings. The T replace the L model and saw changes to steering wheel design, cabin fittings and seat trims.

Of note, the semi-automatic, four-speed 'Sportomatic' transmission was offered for the first time on the flat-six-engined range.

Sheer, simple 3.0-litre style.

Did it dilute the 911's essential rightness? Enthusiasts didn't think so and the type found many converts. A special 911R racer was fitted with a Sportomatic gearbox and won a race!

1968 saw larger wheel arches, wheelbase alterations, twin batteries, revised electrics and quartz-halogen headlamps all arriving, as did a 'comfort' kit for the lower-range 911 which added upgraded trim quality and air horns among its offerings By 1969 the 911E injection landed and so too did the usual round of specification enhancements. A new design of alloy wheel (Fuchs) was a noteworthy upgrade for late 1968. The 911 S – also mechanically fuel injected – now exceeded 150bhp by some margin. A self-levelling front strut suspension option was also available. Reconfiguration of the rear suspension also took place

Such works paved the way for the true upgrades that arrived the 1970s: the 2.2-litre and the 2.7-litre engines.

The 2.2-litre 911 framed the C series of factory developments to the range. The larger, more tractable engine was applied even to the base model 911 for the 1970 model year (production beginning in late 1969). The extra cubic capacity stemmed from the rebore that increased the cylinder bore from 80mm to 84mm. What was less publicized was the change in the geometry to the front suspension struts in a significant tooling alteration that saw a 0.5in/55mm forward movement to improve handling. Part-galvanization of the car (floorpan) started in 1970. Twin circuit braking was added with light alloy calipers for the top models, E and S. Cars for the American market received thicker, more substantial rubber inserts on the front and rear bumper and the addition of hefty over-riders.

Porsche almost left the 911 alone for a year but the 1971 model year saw the arrival of the 2.4-litre engines. The 911 now touched 190bhp and performance really was the key ingredient.

The 1970s body shell in steel remained untouched, with only the bumpers, spoilers, trims and mechanicals modified. 911's basic shape would remain the same for over twenty years. The only noteworthy tooling change during the 2.4 model's production was the removal of the external oil filler and its access flap – in 1973 finally to be hidden and no longer mistaken for a petrol cap.

The mid-1970s saw the key models in the 911's early life story. 1971–3 saw the 2,341cc or 2.4-litre-badged cars develop (as E series) with more performance and more luxurious specifications. The 911S now topped 147mph/230kph and really needed the air dam it deployed under the front end. Soon, the air dam was used across the range. A stronger gearbox was required to handle the increased torque and Porsche did much work on the internal workings of the gearbox which resulted in a revised gear pattern for the driver. The 911 had been transformed into a proper performance car: 0–60mph/120kph in 6.2 seconds was serious stuff, as was that near-150mph/235kph top speed.

The 1970s fashion for black paint and black trim manifested with black-painted front air vents and black finished badging. Soon, black window trims would become fashionable, as would a range of very bright colours with blue, orange and yellow being popular 911 choices at this time. The 2.4-series cars were force-fed their fuel, but the 911T retained a carburettor system in Europe but fuel injection for the American market. Bosch K- Jetronic fuel injection would be used on the next engine to be seen under the 911's bodywork: the 2.7 litre. A limited series of 2.7-litre cars was test-produced and delivered in late 1972.

2.7 Carrera

The next key model in the 911's life was the 2.7 litre that ran from 1973–7. These were the G-series models with the old T and E model variants terminated. In their place came the 150bhp base 911 without any

Targas looked good in white with black roll hoop although many preferred the stainless steel.

added suffix – akin to the first 911. Then came the 175bhp S model. A new range-topper revived the Carrera name previously seen on the 356. This 911 was fitted with a 210bhp engine, mechanical fuel injection, the first deployment of the 'ducktail' rear spoiler, special graphics down the sides of the car and revised technical and trim specifications. That new rear spoiler was neither a styling tweak nor a marketing trick: it was a vital scientifically proven addition. The new rear spoiler and revised integral front air dam worked to reduce the 911's aerodynamic lift at high speed, a reduction of over 60 percent.

The 2,687cc 2.7 Carrera became (from 1972) a famous model. Then came the 2.7 RS series in a fanfare of new trims, colours, badges, fittings and technical improvements. Of note was the use of thinner steel, lightweight panels, plastic valances and thinner-gauged window glass and the glass-fibre engine lid with integral spoiler. Larger Nikasil-coated cylinder liners added capacity to the lighter engine-build specifications and the engine revved to beyond 7,000rpm, Nearly 190lb/ft of torque was on offer and it was delivered in a linear manner, not a peak of power followed by a fall-off or performance. So 2.7 RS really drove and delivered 0–60mph in just over 5 seconds! Larger, 7in rear wheels assisted the handling as did stiffer suspension and gas-filled dampers.

A 2.7 RSH specification was built, with H for race homologation, to fit the rules and 500 RS versions were quickly sold before that figure doubled in a matter of months.

Often delivered in white paint with blue or red side decals and matching Fuchs wheels, Carrera RS defined the 911, its past and its potential. Here was the lightweight 'flyer' before 911 got heavier and, eventually, larger and less nimble.

That rear spoiler and new one-piece synthetic moulded front and rear bumper valances were very obvious new styling and aerodynamic parts fitted to these early 1970s cars as the 2.7-litre RS sports package cars. Sport and touring versions were offered. RS or RSL (L for lightweight) meant much to Porsche fanatics and still does. The RSL versions, unlike the standard production Touring RS, were paired down with thinner gauges, deleted equipment and reduced cabin trims and comforts; even interior door handles were removed to save weight. According to the Porsche technical and restoration experts at Autofarm, these cars weighed around 920kg.

A 2.8-litre RSR variant became the circuit-champion version of the RS theory. Dr Norbert Singer was the man responsible for the RSR development project at Porsche. RSR had flared wheel arches for its wider track and wheels and an increased ride height. The racing versions had slotted air vents incorporated into the flared front and rear wings.

Ultimately a 'high-tailed', heavily modified Carrera RSR 2.14 and then the 1976 2.8-litre Turbo Group 5 racer with a massive and adjustable rear aerofoil topped the 911 racing developments

Early development of the 3.0-litre and turbocharged engines took place under the motor sports division, and via Carrera 3.0-litre RS variations in the Group 3 and then Group 4 racing categories.

The most obvious step-change to 911 would be the fitting of heavy US impact regulation 'big' bumpers with external matt-black bellows. There would also be expensive structural retooling under the skin in order to mount such bumpers into the existing structure. The 1974 model year saw the debut of the somewhat ungainly big bumper series cars. A touch of 911 purity had been lost.

You could also purchase a Carrera variant without all the spoilers and fittings, but it was the be-spoilered type that became iconic. By June 1977, at the height of these new 911 years, Porsche had produced its 250,000th car, with almost 150,000 being 911s.

1974 would see the fitting of the new Porsche-design, high-backed, 'tombstone' seats with integral headrest and exaggerated side bolsters. In 1975/76 Porsche made its usual tweaks or 'continuous improvements'. From trims, to gear ratios, to heating and heaters, from badges to wheels to electric windows, lights and instruments, all were

Guards red, black Targa roll hoop and Turbo body identify this essential 911 Targa.

improved. The shiny 'silver' stainless steel trim on the Targa's B-pillar roll hoop was at this time changed to a matt-black finish – very 1970s.

Soon, to celebrate 911's sporting achievements, you could buy a 911 with 'Martini' stripes, just as you can today. The 2.7-litre engine was phased out for the 1975 model year, yet was still available into 1976 in certain tropical overseas markets. But 2.7-litre was about to give way to the new age of the 911: 3.0-litre power, and a more muscular character. Underneath however, there lay much of the original 911's 1963 body and metal.

930 Turbo

The first 911 as a 'Turbo' arrived for 1975. It would soon be cited as the 930 series but the early 1975/76 cars were less obvious about being Germany's fastest car. Here was the 2,996cc- or 3.0-litre engine with 260bhp and wider rear track and bodywork with revised spoilers and trims. Porsche had only really intended to register the car for racing and build 500 units, but the marketing department soon realized the car's potential – even if BMW's turbocharged cars had proved unreliable at this time.

The 911 Turbo range would last from 1975 through to the 1990s in its initial guises, before being re-interpreted for the late 1990s. The early 3.0-litre and post-1988 3.3-litre cars needed intelligent driving and some level of concentration in comparison to normally aspirated 911s.

Porsche produced thirty examples of a pure racer based on the 911 but confusingly tagged 934. Private buyers could purchase a 485bhp tuned-up 934 and go racing. Ultimately 620bhp was offered by Porsche's racing department.

By the end of 1976 only one 2.7 model remained as Porsche announced its 3.0-litre, 200bhp new standard engine. The turbocharged Turbo models of 260bhp had arrived, and with them came a raft of trim and specification changes. Of note, a less brittle aluminium crankcase replaced the magnesium item previously used (the bore casings on the larger-bored engine were thinner and magnesium was subject to cracking, as also found in aerospace applications). Across the range, the 911 now received full-body zinc galvanization which was to greatly improve the car's rust resistance. Use of zinc-coated steel (on both sides/surfaces of the panels) marked another step upwards in 911 quality. Further gearbox developments (Type 915 and beyond) were necessary as power and torque increased.

The debut of the Turbo cars took the 911 into a new league; it also took 911 into new handling challenges and larger rear wheels, 'wide-body' rear panels, and aerodynamic additions were all deployed to try and tame the potentially wayward behaviours with all that power. 911 was now capable of well over 150mph and had true supercar performance. From 911 to 911 Turbo, the car entered a new era, amid new specifications and a new look inside and out.

In 1978 the 911 SC replaced the 911 standard model and the Carrera 3.0 litre. The Turbo branding took over amid a 930 series definition. Here came the 'tea-tray' rear spoiler, the 'whale-tail' rear spoiler, the wide rear track and bodywork, de-chroming, vibrant new seat trims and cabin colours, better air conditioning, new door mirror designs, and a complete revamp. 911 put on weight but it also put on power and ability.

Porsche dealt with Turbo car's turbocharger 'lag', which occurs when the exhaust gases are not spinning-up the turbocharger (throttle off), by tuning the exhaust pipe's back pressure via a special flap – this reduced the pressure acting against the non-charged (throttle off) turbo, and reduced inertia in the turbo by reducing the intake pipe 'back' pressure. It did not, as some thought, 'pre-charge' the turbocharger and its turbine; that was a development that was years away.

The turbocharged cars had in excess of of 250lb/ft of torque at a low 4,000rpm – this really put strain on certain components and Porsche had to design a new drivetrain with a tougher gearbox and larger flywheel and clutch. Only four speeds were offered in this gearbox until 1988 when a fifth gear was added. Latterly, Porsche would fit Pirelli

The 911 964 series was a re-engineered, stronger, safer 911 yet did not look 'new'. Nevertheless it reached its height in the magnesium-'cup'-wheeled RS series of 1991/92 as shown here. 120kg lighter and with a few more horsepower at 260bhp, this 3.6 litre really flew. The (40mm lower) ride was, shall we say, 'firm'. Zero to 60mph in less than 5.4 seconds was on offer. Christian Ayres owns this car and several other 911s.

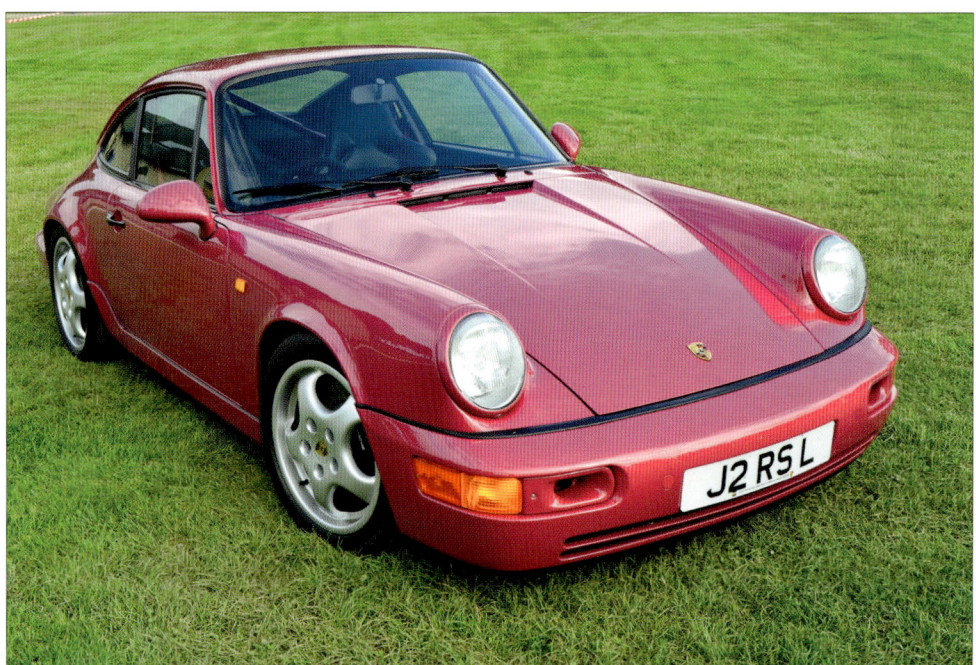

P-series tyres to great effect and make some chassis/suspension changes to try and 'tame' the Turbo's fearsome reputation.

The Turbo cars could hit 60mph in under five seconds, storm to 160mph and fly sideways if mishandled by a novice. But 930 Turbo was to become the 1980s supercar fantasy for many schoolboys and grown men alike. Lower down the range, the 911 SC Sport, and the Carrera 3.0 litre all benefitted from the raft of technical and specification improvements. A 'narrow'-body 3.2-litre 911 SC fitted with the new aerofoil rear spoiler, de-chromed trim and air-conditioning, proved to be a popular interpretation. The very rare non-turbocharged 1984 911 Carrera SC/RS was faster than a Turbo and of very light weight, with only twenty built.

For 1983, Porsche did something unexpected: it removed the 911's traditional front end and fitted a modern 'flat-nose' front with concealed 'pop-up' headlamps. This was more like the racing 935-series 911 modifications, and it was modern and more aerodynamic, had less cross-wind effects and was technically clever, yet it looked wrong in many people's eyes and sold as a factory 'special' in limited numbers. By 1985, a flat-nose SE with wider wheels and over 300bhp was offered: it could reach 175mph, assisted by its better aerodynamic penetration.

One of the most interesting 911s of this era had to be the rare 3.2-litre Clubsport variant. This car featured a 100kg weight saving by having much interior trim (including the rear seats) stripped out. Here was a return to a purer 911 experience.

At this time Porsche created the 911 Cabriolet; a soft-top, weather-proof, fold-down roof really added a new lease of life to the 911. But chopping the roof off affected the structure and weighty reinforcements were needed. The aerodynamics suffered too: hood up or down and the rear wing's beneficial downforce was reduced by the soft-top effect.

Targa and Cabriolet versions of the Turbo range were announced in 1986. The 911 Speedster of 1987 saw even the windscreen A-pillars chopped off and a lightweight and low-height windscreen replace it. A special rear deck cover added to the restyle as 911 aped the old 35 Speedster look. Under 200 were sold. It would continue as part of the

Carrera 2 range with the wide-body Turbo-look Speedster; just over 2,000 would sell as the 1990s arrived, but the 911 Speedster was perhaps more about marketing than design.

Despite its legend the truth was that by the 1980s the 911, however well tweaked and modified, was underneath it all, an old car dating from the 1960s. The last of the 930 Turbos was gone by the end of 1989. Overall, 911 sales began declining as cheaper and easier-to-own rivals came to the fore. Porsche needed to act.

959

959 was Porsche's attempt to create a 1980s new-age supercar but it did so by taking the core chassis/body shell of the 911 and creating a composite-bodied, four-wheel drive, 'active' ride height hypercar at vast expense. Conceived at the height of the Group B racing specification era, 959 capitalized on such investment in that potential by creating a new Porsche hallmark for the mid-1980s.

A development chassis 959 won the Paris–Dakar rally in 1984 before 959 went on sale in 1986; 959 raced all over the place and did well at Le Mans, but ultimately it was a technology showcase for what Porsche could do.

The man behind Project B was Helmuth Bott, Porsche's great engineer of the 911 era. The man who led the engineering development of the car was Manfred Bantle. Styling was by the Porsche design group under Anatole Lapine. Lapine, a huge race and rally fan, was close to the 959 and spent time modifying the clay styling model as it developed to its final form in 1985. Roland Kussmaul was 959's lead development engineer. The 959's lead-test engineer and development driver was Dieter Röscheisen who did much of the development work on the braking and drivetrain systems. Uwe Makrutzki was a technical lead.

Fitted with the greatest development of the flat-six engine, the 959's power unit was 'stroked', as the American's say, with Group C racing technology. Offering 450bhp as a 2.8-litre twin-turbocharged (sequential ratios), force-fed quad cam (yet perfectly ventilated and cooled) engine happy to burble along in traffic, with aluminium/magnesium engine castings and titanium rods and crank, this was the air-cooled engine taken to its zenith but in fact had water-cooled heads! Four valves per cylinder and four camshafts, twin inter-coolers, air-cooled cylinders and extra cooling form a water-cooled head jacket, started by Bosch electronic ignition and fuel feed, all signalled sheer engineering intent from Porsche. Much had been learned from the 956–962 racing programme and the engine modifications found to be possible.

The 959's key engineering features were the Porsche-Steuer Kupplung (PSK) or clutch control mechanism system as

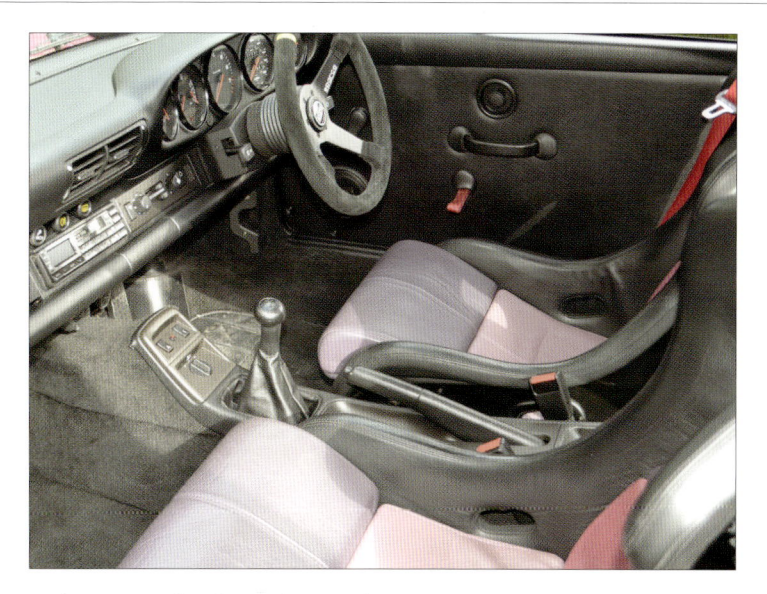

964 RS interior offered special seats and trims.

964 RS engine bay in all its originality.

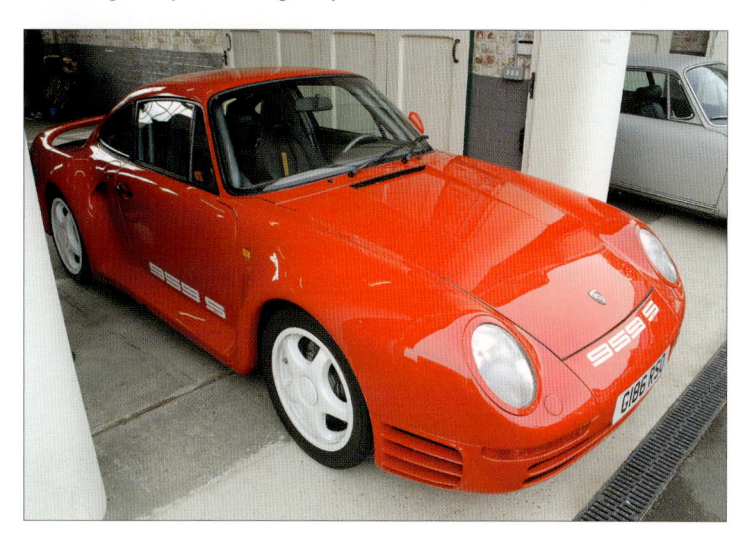

the most sophisticated four-wheel drive mechanism ever dreamed up. PSK was the only system which could vary the front-to-rear torque-split percentage under normal operating parameters

The advanced aerodynamics (C_D 0.31) functioned well despite the steep angle of the old 911's glass house which formed the basis of the car's centre section. 959 was

The 959 in its Sport iteration. Here was a true landmark in the 911 story that began with the Group B racing series and ended up in a four-wheel-drive, hi-tech supercar.

26 PORSCHE 911: CLASSIC GERMAN SPORTS CAR

Porsche rear spoiler development and styling passed through several eras. Achieving the compromise between drag, lift reduction, side angle efficiency and engine cooling required much thought. The 911 Targa and 911 Cabriolet on show.

Above: The 993 (1993–8) was a radical update and looked 'newer' than 964's update. Purists can argue the details amongst themselves. 959 styling traits are not invisible.

Right: The 933 also introduced a very clever sliding-roof Targa top as seen here. Just be sure no water accumulates behind the back seat!

truly a technological force. The body was of composite Kevlar-layered construction of outer panels amid a steel core.

With 200 customer deposits (DM50,000 each) taken for a road-going version (to be called 959), Porsche would spend the next three years battling to turn the car into production reality. It went on sale in 1986. On offer were 'Komfort' and 'Sport' models, with prices starting at DM431,000. Just under 300 production-sales status 959s were made (people argue over figures of 283 or 292).

959 was 911 taken to the extreme, but much of its technology would filter down into Porsche.

New era: 964 to 993

Porsche could not afford to develop a new 911 from the ground up, so instead, for the launch in the 1988 model year, it took the inner pressings of the existing 911, kept the front and rear side window designs, and reinforced the body shell with new sills, rails and new metals. Completely new front and rear bumper sections and light shapes gave the car a modern feel. Yet it looked very familiar.

Under the skin came coil-spring suspension, revised engines, a four-wheel-drive option and, latterly, a Turbo version. Shaped by Anatole Lapine's studio, the completely re-engineered 964 had two figures in the background: Norbert Singer oversaw the aerodynamic developments, and Wolfgang Möbius and the Australian designer Richard Soderberg drew the new shapes. 964 truly was the 911 comprehensively reworked in an all-new body yet which retained the vital window graphics and roof shape. It was stronger, safer, more stylish, more modern and easier and safer to drive.

This was the 964 series 911 of post-1989. By 1993 it could be had as 360bhp, 3.6-litre Turbo 3.6 with a top speed that could nudge 180mph.

Initially launched with four-wheel drive, latterly with two-wheel drive (and better for it, said some), 964 changed the character of

Left: Riveria Blue 993: just add VarioRam and it'll fly...

Below: 993 GT2 race specification: a stunning example about to race up Prescott Hill Climb.

the 911: it was more refined and less pure and, even in Turbo form, less raw. This might have offended purists but it increased sales to customers old and new.

Key variants included the Carrera 4 and Carrera 2: both featured an automatically deploying rear 'wing' that raised itself up and acted as a lift dumper or spoiler to make the car more stable at higher speeds; it was no gimmick and it also forced cooling air into the engine bay and oil cooler.

964 in its first version as a four-wheel-drive car was tuned for safety and actually understeered – classic 911s oversteered and this took some getting used to: technology had intervened.

964 evolved across the years and was more reliable, more rust-resistant and more crashworthy than its ancestor. Yet it felt as if a little bit of the original 911 magic it was missing. The four-wheel-drive car was of less direct steering and feel, but enthusiasts soon warmed to the rear-wheel-drive variant which seemed to evoke more of the classic 911 spirit. This car was over 100kg lighter without its four-wheel-drive mechanicals and much nicer to steer.

Developments include the semi-automatic Tiptronic gearbox for the Carrera 2 only, a Targa version and of course a Speedster of which less than 1,000 were built.

One of the vital 964 models was the RS, a high-powered version with reduced weight (removing the air conditioning, underbody sealing and some electrical items) but with a luxury-trimmed interior with Recaro seats and also delivering massive performance: only very hard ride settings caused reactions from 'old school' Porsche fans. A great car, but certainly not a rebirth of the original 1973 Carrera RS. As late as 1992/93, Porsche produced a 964 Turbo S Lightweight. Only eighty-six were constructed and the car featured extra air inlets front and rear to aid cooling.

993

As 1990 ended, Porsche remained troubled by slow sales and few models. All its supercar eggs lay in one basket: 911. The 924 and 928 had proved to be brilliant but they were not 911. Former Porsche designer, the Dutchman Harm Laagy (Laagij) returned to work at Porsche and realized that a deep-seated and true update to the 911 concept was required. He came up with very substantial visual changes to the body of the 911. Even though the side window design was retained, the 993 had radical new front and rear sections of wider and sculpted design. Major technical work took place underneath its skin. In some senses it resembled the Porsche 959 hyper car and in others it set a wonderful new, up-to-date style that was of significant effect. The interior was also revised.

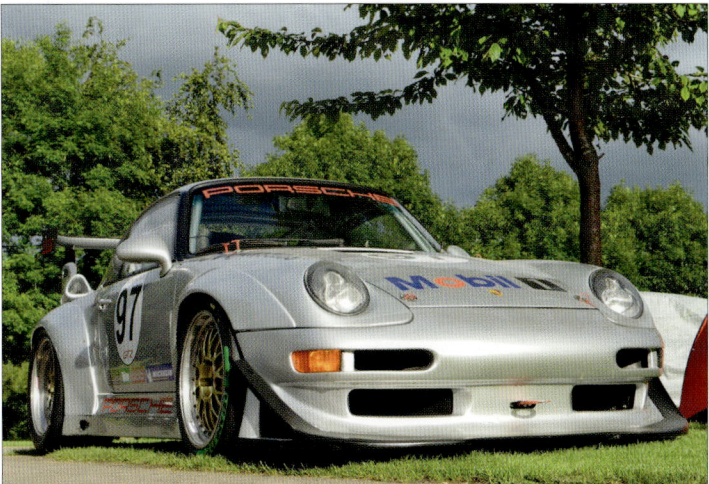

In 993, Porsche ended its semi-trailing arm rear suspension and created a contemporary multilink set up. A six-speed gearbox greatly aided high-speed cruising and the electronic semi-automatic Tiptronic was further developed into a smoother-operating mechanism. Anti-lock brakes were updated and so too were the wheel designs. Porsche also introduced its Varioram variable intake timing and induction system with the 993, bringing great efficiency to the combustion and sparking process within the engine.

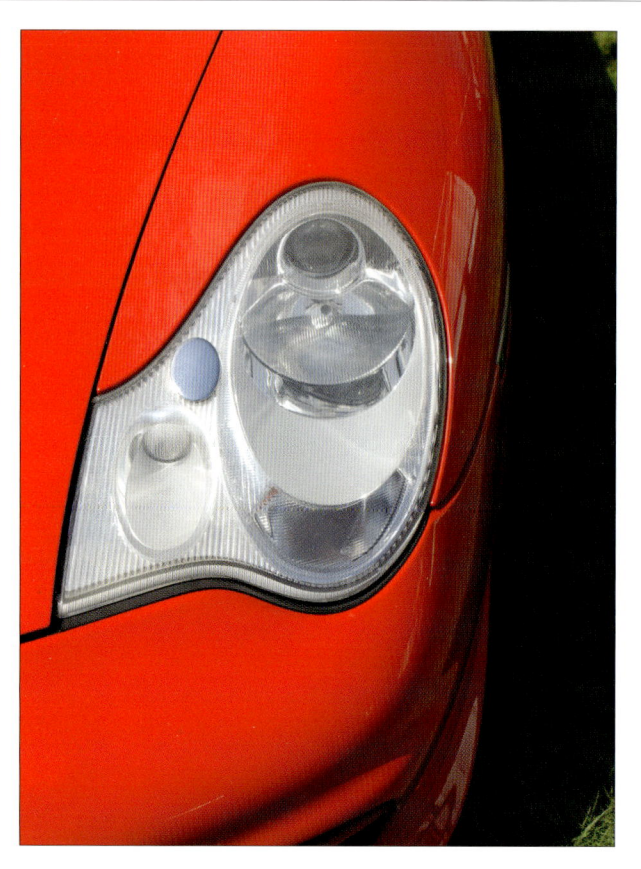

Top left: Porsche design language: 993 Turbo with the later rear-spoiler design sculpture. Pure Porsche! Make it a 993 Turbo S and all you will see is a blur.

Top right: The water-cooled 996 came in from 1996 and was revised with this new headlamp design motif from 2001.

993 also created a completely new Targa model with a clever glass roof that slid backwards and downwards. Its rear side windows were a different, sharper shape, too. A true cabriolet was also offered. 993 as top-of-the-range 3.6-litre Turbo featured wide-bodied rear styling and side skirts. 993 also featured perhaps the ultimate development of the Porsche (static) rear spoiler design work after many hours of wind tunnel experimentation.

In 993, the legend of Carrera RS came back with a bite and also evolved into an RS Clubsport variant as a heavily spoilered – actually 'winged' – car of massive performance. Of note, the 993 four-wheel-drive C4 type had a viscous rather than a mechanical differential coupling which seemed to bring great improvement to the driving of the car. Forty percent of the power could be automatically fed to the front wheels if a loss of grip was sensed by the system. This was the best development so far of the four-wheel-drive system as applied to 911.

993 RS was a 300bhp car and it drove wonderfully even if it did have power steering. 993 also provided a Turbo and a GT2 model. These really were hard-core machines and featured bolt-on bodywork extensions to cover wider wheels and tyres, biplane rear wings, roll cage and full competition equipment. Over 400bhp was on tap. This factory car soon usurped the 'Specials' built up from the 911s as racing cars and street-legal racers by numerous European tuning houses. Zero to 60mph in 3.6 seconds made GT2 rather effective. A GT2 R 'Evo' version topped the racing-specification 993 GT series.

996

Despite 993's sales success, and the slow improvement to reception for the front-engined 'transaxle' Porsche of 924, 944 and 928, Porsche still had huge operating costs and a narrow sales base. The company was in fact facing a crisis. What it needed to do was launch a new, volume-sales base model and a new 911.

Porsche management took the decision to develop a new two-seat soft-top (the Boxster) and a totally new 911. Both cars would share 33 percent of their parts and be almost identical in structural and under-the-skin tooling, from the B-pillars forward to the nose. This 'shared commonality' 911 was to be called the 996 series. Critically, it would step away from air-cooling and use a water-cooled engine (but still a flat-six). Purists were horrified, but here was a car that was cheaper to build, had more profit in it and which would be a totally new look for 911.

Syled by Hong Kong-born 'Pinky Lai' in Haarm Laagy's Porsche studio, the car developed the curves of the 993 into a new style and effectively modernized a line of 911s that had shared the same shape and the same side windows and roof panel since the 1960s. Finally, however controversial to the purists, 911 was a new car for a new age.

With a six-cylinder boxer engine with dual overhead cams, four valves per head, Porsche's refined variable intake timing system and hydraulic adjusters, this engine was pure Porsche even if it was water-cooled.

Despite its water-cooling, 996 sounded like a Porsche, drove like a 911 should

Variations on a Theme 29

Left: This earlier 997 'full fat' variant has the right decals and a biplane rear wing.

Below: The revised face of the 996 displays the bodywork specification differences that evolved. Plenty of air went in through the larger front vents.

and was stronger and safer than ever. The headlamp design was a major departure from traditional 911 design but nowhere near as controversial as some suggest. A swept cabin turret and roof got the 'aero' drag rating down to an impressive $C_D 0.30$.

Launched in 1997 for the 1998 model year, the 3,387cc 3.4-litre 911 as the 996 series was bigger, and different – but it had to be to meet all the new legislation that car makers faced. The car topped 170mph and did 0–60mph in just over 5 seconds. Most buyers loved the new car, but it did develop some issues with engine wear which affected its reputation somewhat and Porsche acted to resolve these problems.

The range developed through to a plethora of models: Carrera 4, C4S, Turbo, twin-turbo GT2 RS, GT2 Clubsport, GT3 and of course a cabriolet. 996 could be specified as a proper, luxury-performance GT car, or as a rawer, 'performance' sports car. The base 'showroom' car offered 300bhp, with the hard-core performance models reaching 483bhp! GT2 offered ceramic brakes for the first time on a Porsche. The Porsche Variocam camshaft/valve intake timing system also appeared on later model 996s.

A special 'Anniversary' 911 jubilee edition packed with performance-pack upgrades and luxury trim was also marketed. 996 gained acceptance and today the performance versions are as respected as other modern 911s.

A revised 996 with altered headlamps and detail improvements was phased in in 2001 but by the close of 2004, the 997-series 911 was waiting in the wings. 996 can be defined as 'Generation 1' and 'Generation 2' across its production life 1998–2005.

997

This series of the 911 addressed some enthusiasts' concerns about the 996. Although using approximately 20 percent of the 996's engineering underpinnings, 997 was a 'back to the future'-type effect in terms of its styling, which reverted to traditional 911 headlamp and light lens shapes. Launched for the 2005 model year in late 2004, here again was a brilliant modern interpretation of the 911 story. But again, it had got bigger and taken a further step away from the original 911's small, lithe character. This was inevitable if the car was to meet modern needs and retain its performance.

Water-cooled, yet with mechanical steering and all the usual Porsche ingredients, the 997 model range echoed the 911 bloodline and offered standard, Turbo, Carrera, S, GT2/Lightweight, GT3

This 997 T (Generation 1) was Porsche Cars Great Britain's press demo car and in Riveria Blue, as it should be. Note the return to more classic 911 design motifs. The rear wing is lovely, and so too was the run up Goodwood's hill where this was taken.

Modern classic: 911 amongst its brothers.

Tale of two tails: 911 elements as captured in raw yellow. Rear wing design again to the fore – or stern.

Below: Later 911 interiors aped the original series without being too 'retro'.

Later 997 in black and on the move – pure 911 driving joy.

and GT3RS variations – right up towards 500bhp and 200mph performance. Many felt that Porsche had recaptured the essence of the 911 story in the 997 as far as was possible and in 3.8-litre Carrera S, GT3 and GT3 RS forms, and finally in the rare 4.0 litre: all received many superlatives from drivers and owners.

997 GT3 also furthered the use of Porsche's electronic systems such as Porsche Active Suspension Management (PASM) which sensed and controlled the suspension dynamics according to road conditions and settings. A six-speed Tiptronic was also offered. Later 997 Turbos were fitted with two turbochargers with sequential settings in order to reduce turbo lag (the VTG system). 997 GT3 RS featured carbon-fibre panels and a plastic rear window – all to reduce weight.

As with 996, the 997 fell into Generation 1 and Generation 2 styling and specification variations in a production life running from late 2004 to 2013. Generation 2 997s from 2008 used the revised 911DFI engine – replacing the 996-series-based M97 engine which had suffered from intermediate shaft issues. The 2008–12 997 C2 S was offered with a new PDK semi-automatic, twin-clutched gearbox. From 2009–12 997s received updated lights, styling, six-piston brake calipers, engine upgrades and a seven-speed manual gearbox.

Variations on a Theme 31

The 991 series (as GT3) with longer wheelbase and reduced rear overhang debuted in 2011 and evolved into 991.2 and into today's latest series. Back to being a hard-core 911.

991

Here was a further redesign on sale from 2011 in 350bhp base 911 model format. Of note, the engine mounting's rear overhang was reduced and the wheelbase lengthened to further refine the handling. The styling was 993-series influenced but in no way 'retro'. The 3.9-litre Carrera 4S touched 185mph and had 400bhp.

Lightweight aluminium construction was used in 30 percent of the 991's construction.

Across 2012–16, 991 evolved into Carrera S, Carrera 4, 4 S, GT3, Turbo, Turbo S (560bhp), Anniversary, GTS, C4 GTS and finally the wide-bodied GT3 RS (493bhp). Significantly the Mezger engine in the GT3 version was replaced with the DFI engine. The cabriolet body option was retained.

Despite its reliance on a raft of electronic devices and interventions, it was a driver's car and performance car: 997 was very popular and re-established the 911 in the minds of the 911 purist and hard-core enthusiasts. GT and Turbo models gained 'rear-steer' technology. A seven-speed gearbox also debuted on the 997 in 2011.

991.2

This post-2015 car added to the 991 with an innovative new engine and gearbox and many technical refinements. Expertly restyled, this 2016-model-year car offered turbocharging across the range via low- and high-pressure model options, rear-wheel steer technology, and a great deal of new engine technology. Of note, two different new engines were used in the 991.2 series: the 3.0-litre 9A2 in the lower models and the 3.8-litre 9A1 in the Turbo models. A 911 R 'homage' would appear in 991 guise at this time and prove very rare and highly prized.

The main challenge for Porsche was to introduce a turbocharged 911 base model without it suffering from the traditional behaviour and perceptions of turbocharged engines. Porsche put a great deal of work into tuning the engine and its

A more subtle choice for a current 911 series is this grey. Revised intakes and subtle development are pure Porsche, but the iconography remains the same.

Green dream: the RS series with louvred front wing-wheel vents and all the 'aero' aids. A bit like flying on the ground.

forced induction system to avoid the peaky turbo pitfalls of old. Even trying to keep the traditional 911 sound was a challenge as turbochargers can effectively quieten and smooth out engine sounds.

The lamp/light designs, notably at the rear, and revised body panels all lent a fresh new look that was modern yet not too revolutionary. But for the first time the base or entry-level 911 was turbocharged. A 3.0-litre, 370bhp flat six with 0.9-bar

Grand Prix Silver with dark red interior trim (leather with alloy accents) was a classy modern choice for this recent 991.2 series Porsche. But there was no doubt that 911 was putting on weight.

intercoolers. The engine featured a fuel pump for each bank of cylinders and a new direct injection system. The old Variocam system to alter valve settings via the camshaft actuation was improved and extended to the exhaust valves. Hugely efficient, with low CO_2 output, this new engine could quite easily deliver in excess of 35mpg when driven carefully. The Porsche Active Suspension Management (PASM) seen across the previous 997 and 991 series was also further refined to alter ride height and roll resistance when required and fitted as standard across the 991.2 range.

Oddly, the new, more efficient 991.2 was over 30kg heavier than the 991.1, which was due to engineering reinforcements in the engine and gearbox.

Highlights of 991-series development included the PDK automatic-only GT, which was finally made available with a manual gearbox.

992

In late 2018 Porsche heavily revised the 911, deployed aluminium panels to 70 percent of the car and evoked some original classic 911 design themes. Upfront came Carrera and Carrera 4 followed by the S variants and the full Carrera 2. The Turbo and GT variants are sure to follow. The standard transmission at launch was the PDK semi-auto system. 992 has no manual gearbox offering to date but it will surely come.

For the first time, 911 was fitted with a full-width moveable rear spoiler that was more of a wing – as opposed to a shorter, traditional spoiler panel. It was also fitted movable front air intakes which could be set to respond to wet-weather driving to provide enhanced aerodynamics. An eight-speed PDK auto-gearbox was also fitted.

Overall, the 992 refined the legacy of the 911 design story and a new emphasis was placed on the rear end of the car in styling terms. In 992, designers Benjamin Baum and Thomas Stopka, overseen by Porsche Studio 992 leader Peter Varga, created a return to cleaner 911 shape. The new cabin design was led by Ivo van Hulten and created a true classic 911 'cockpit' effect with a clever interpretation of the historic 911 instrument cluster and horizontal or transverse lines across the fascia. The new age of digital connection and displays are now integrated into the 911 cabin.

The engines have refined direct injection and continued development of the famous variable intake system. For 2019 the Carrera 2 and 4S and a C4S cabriolet further evolved the body style and extended the range. The Turbo and GT3 await as 992 looks forward and also back across eight generations of the 911 – still the most desirable GT sports car and still the most desirable classic car.

pressure ratio setting was allocated to the standard 911, while the Carrera S had 1.1-bar pressure ratio for its forced induction charger and 420bhp. These were smaller, more responsive turbos that did not need the previously used complication of variable turbine blade settings. Both engines delivered a very large increase in usable torque and at lower revs – aiding drivability. But it was not a breathless, turbocharged all-or-nothing engine: the rev limit was up above 7,500rpm. A twin-plate clutch was fitted.

Massive amounts of cooling air were forced into the engine bay to feed the turbochargers and to aid cooling via two

Motor Sport Legend

The Porsche Historika – truly a historic 901-series car – poses as it enters a corner at Goodwood. Only 232 901-series 911s were built; this one is a 1964 car chassis 3000241. It was previously owned and raced by F. F. Kozka and competitively driven by Walter Rohrl, and more recently driven by Rowan Atkinson.

Below: The recent 991-series GT2RS in racing-style specification can also be driven on the road as a daily driver. Note adjustable, high-downforce rear wing and front wheel arch outflow vents.

No review of the 911 story can be without reference to its motor sport history across everything from circuit racing, rallying, hill climbing and other incarnations of competition. Here we briefly look at the 911 competitive driving story because it is an essential ingredient and outcome of what the 911 was and what it did. Traction, power and handling, allied to nimbleness and size, were the key to the 911's success.

Porsche men from the 356/550/718 era had laid down the ethos of Porsche rally and race success. The greats included Edgar Barth, Jean Behra, Constantin Berkheim, Joakim Bonnier, Fritz Huschke von Hanstein, Hans Herrman, Hans Klauser, Herbert Linge, Peter Mueller, Richard von Frankenburg Prince von Metternich, Berghe von Tripps, Wolfgang von Tripps, Dan Gurney and we should not forget that Stirling Moss also drove for Porsche, notably in the 718RS61.

To this day, classic 911s, old and new, scream or howl up hills – even at decades-old tracks like Prescott. Silverstone and Goodwood events see 911s racing in all-out competitions across the annual events calendar. All these years on, Richard Attwood is still racing 911s. Tony Dron achieved many successes driving various 911s across the pre-millennium racing calendar. Ex-Formula One drivers, right up to Mark Webber, drive Porsches on the road and for races. From 1965 to date, Porsches, notably 911s, have been the choice of many champions.

GT2RS hunkered down and in Miami Blue - showing off the major aerodynamic revisions to the 991- series body, notably the rear wing and engine lid intakes and vents. Not to be trifled with even by Italian hypercars.

Right: Shades of the Martini-liveried 'Le Mans' 930s, but a race-specification 911 RS going up Prescott. Phil Price of Connaught Engineering is the driver and operator.

Below: Early-series purism at Goodwood. This is the ex-Vic Elford 911 and is a 1968 SWB ex-Porsche GB press demo car, latterly owned by Nick Faure. Note the cabin 'cage' and steering wheel. Soon to start up and scream like only an air-cooled 911 can on the cam.

Owners love using their classic 911s; in this case David Strange goes up Prescott. These are not cars to be preserved in aspic.

Similar activities take place across America, Europe and the Far East.

The first 911s were used in German and French rallies within three months of the car's 1964 launch. Porsche 911 man Herbert Linge with co-driver Peter Falk came fifth at the 1965 Monte Carlo Rally in, race number 147. Porsche's Norbert Singer was the man responsible for racing Carreras, Vic Elford and co-driver David Stone won the 1967 Tour of Corsica in a 911R. They also won the 1967 Lyon–Charbonnière Rally in their 911 and the Tulip and the Geneva rallies in 1967. Elford co-drove a 911 Sportomatic with J. Neerpach and H. Herrman to win the Marathon de la Route of 1967. Elford would win the 1968 Monte Carlo Rally, H. Toivonen would come second – both in 911s of course.

Gérard Larrousse won the same race in a 911 in 1969 and won the Tour de France that year in a 911. A 911 won the 1967 Spa 24 Hours race at the hands of driver Gaban. B. Waldegaard (with Elmer) won the 1969 Monte Carlo Rally in a 911S. Vic Elford and David Stone came second in their 911S. Hans Herrman took the 911 to the East African Safari as early as 1968. (The 911 won the 1968 World Rally Championship, and was second overall in the East African Rally of 1974.

In 1968, a 911 won the GT race at Watkins Glenn with Gregg and Everett driving. Gregg and Huth won the GT race at the Nürburgring. Also in 1968, a 911 triumphed in the GT class at Le Mans, driven by Gaban and Schutz.

From 1966 to 1975, the 911 stormed to race, rally and hill-climb victories across the motor sport calendar. From the GT at Monza to the Targa Florio, over all the main FIA rallies in Sweden, Greece and beyond, 911 triumphed. 911 took World Rally Championships in 1968, 1970, and also took the 1973 European Championship. In America, the Penske organization campaigned various 911s with success.

Gérard Larrousse drove the lightest-ever 911 – the rally-specification 911 ST he used in the 1970 Tour de France. It weighed 780kg (just over 1,700lb). It came home in second place.

911 – notably as RSR 3.0-litre – took ten national championship races in 1974 alone and the 1975 IMSA National Championship (USA) in 1975. John Fitzpatrick took the RSR to first in the GT class Le Mans 24

Motor Sport Legend 35

Left: In the pits: 911 time warp at the Aldington Cup race at Goodwood Members; Day ... rev, rev, rev.

Below: Recent 911 race-specification sees all manner of addenda and some very nice vinyl!

Below centre: Three generations of 911s ready for hill-climb action. You can almost smell the things.

Hours in 1975. Le Mans would be where the heavily modified RSR 911s and 911 derivatives would perhaps be most visible.

Early 911 Race highlights included:
1969 Le Mans 24 Hours: winner. Porsche 911: Daytona GT 24 Hours: winner Porsche 911
1970 Nürburgring GT 1,000km: winner Porsche 911
1971 Le Mans 24 Hours: winner GT Class, Porsche 911 RSR
1972 European GT Trophy: winner Porsche 911
1973 Dijon 1,000km: winner GT Class, Porsche Carrera RSR Group 4 GT
1973 Daytona 24 Hours: winner, Porsche 911 Carrera RSR
1974 Le Mans: 2nd overall, Porsche 911 Carrera 2.14T
1975 Daytona 24 Hour: winner, Porsche 911 Carrera RSR

Well-known 911 rally/race drivers:

A. Andersson	G. Larrousse
R. Attwood	G. Klass
E. Barth	H. Linge
D. Bell	H. Muller
V. Elford	W. Rohrl
P. Falk	R. Stommelen
J. Fitzpatrick	D. Stone
G. Follmer	H. Toivonen
P. Frere	R. Tuthill
P. Gregg	G. van Lennep
H. Haywood	B. Waldegaar
H. Hermann	

We should not forget that a development chassis 959 won the Paris–Dakar Rally in 1984 and 1986.

The Porsche 961 – developed from the 911/959 – proved successful, notably at Le Mans in 1986, winning the GTX Class and attaining seventh overall. 911s are still winning amateur, club and national events to this day with the Porsche-sponsored 911 Cup series being very much to the fore and globally televized.

911 still rules.

The essential mid-1970s Porsche 935 racer with rare long tail and based on much-modified 911 / 935 / 77 underpinnings. The aero front inspired the later flat-nose 911 variant.

36 PORSCHE 911: CLASSIC GERMAN SPORTS CAR

The thin-section wheels and pure nature of the 911's original scale are shown here with added front bumper over-riders fitted. Keeping the 356-style podded headlamps and separate front wing line was a decision that proved to be timeless in its effect.

Porsche undertook many experiments to get the rear engine lid vent to the correct and most efficient design. This drawing depicts the rear over-riders that were soon added to the early 911s. Note the vents at the top of the rear windscreen and the original narrow body style.

The classic early 2.0-litre 911 profile and front and rear aspects reveal the ellipsoid shapes and perfect scaling of the design by F.A. 'Butzi' Porsche – as launched in 1964. Prior to main series production, the fuel filler cap was re-shaped and a thin chrome strip added to the sill-line. The 901-series name became the defining 911. Pressed steel wheels ceased to be available on 911 after 1974.

Seen from above, 911's long fastback roof section can be seen to dominate the scale of the car, yet not in an unbalanced manner. Recent versions of the 911 legend have had shorter noses and longer and wider rear bodies that some feel have unbalanced the car's lines. This early-series 911 shows off the perfect proprotions and the rounded and chamfered corners, the rear deck and the prominent front wing lines from the characteristic headlamps, flowing back into the classic 911 wing-to-windscreen pillar hip-line join. Early 911 was quite delicate. Adding big bumpers and wider rear wings changed the shape of the car.

The effect of the larger 5-mph US specification bumpers and revised front airdam and valance are obvious in this front view of a 1970s 911 SC. However, the main body pressings and glass remained the same as the original 911. Extras included headlamp washers, a new rear wing, and, in 1987, a rare white-only Carrera Club Sport 'CS' version. 189 were built including claims of one in Targa specification. A US–specification variant was also made for the US market only.

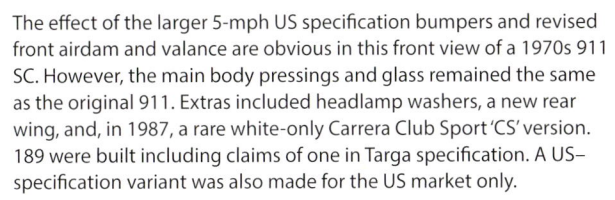

Revised rear bodywork and lamps, bigger bumpers and better aerodynamics and differing rear wing line all mark out the later version of the classic 911 as seen here in the 3.0-litre SC variant.

The classic US-specification big bumper mid-1970s to mid-1980s 911 complete with 'cheese cutter' alloy wheels and rear over-riders. With fully galvanized body, added luxury trim items and available across 2.7- then 3.0-litre capacities, this was the car that carved out a new niche for Porsche, notably as the SC Sport model variant. Side-door impact bars were added, as were headlamp washers, a rear wing, and in 1987 a rare white-only Carrera Club Sport CS version. One hundred and eighty-nine were built including claims of one in Targa specification.

The subtle lines of the small bumper, short wheelbase earlier pre-1970 911 shell in basic trim. Such cars weighed around 1,050kg according to specification. Later cars of G-series might weigh up to 1,500kg. Cars with the 221cm wheelbase used a cover over the rear torsion bar access point, whereas in the 227cm-wheelbase car, the rear wheelarch was moved backward and the sill extended behind the access panel.

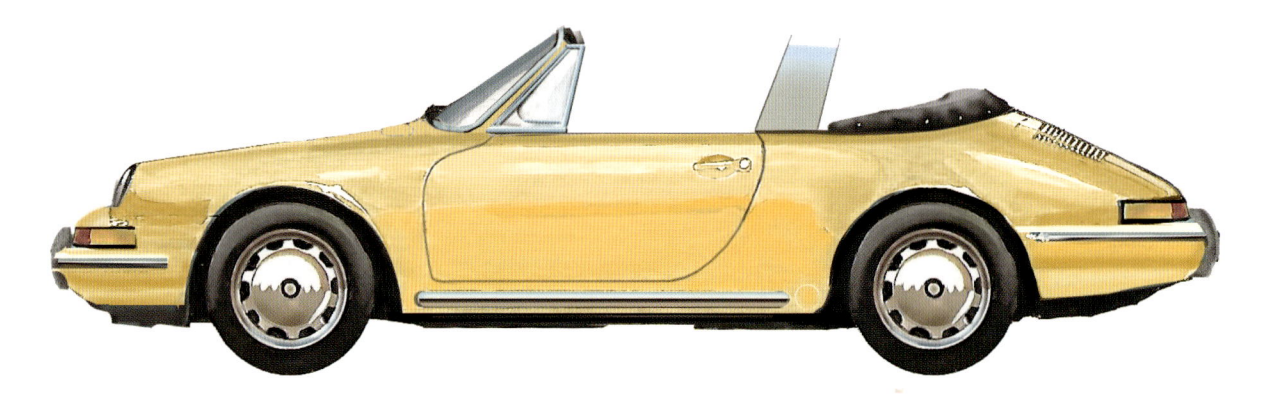

This is the essence of Targa based on the early A-series 911 Targa introduced in August 1967 and depicted here with the rare, fold-down canvas/perspex rear roof/window section which was of short production run prior to the fixed, glass wraparound rear window becoming standard fitting for the 1969 model year. The lift-out Targa roof panel was stored in a special slipcase. Of note, low-numbers of 912 Targa variants were also produced. The polished alloy B-pillar trim was in later 1970s models, and painted black. Targa lives on today and the polished alloy-clad B-pillar is back.

The classic early 1970s 149mph 2.7 RS Carrera series launched the ducktail rear deck spoiler and the age of a lighter 911 (with more power and with decals available). Most production RS had colour-keyed wheels that were a close match to the red or blue side decal options. Lightweight body panels of alloy and thinner-gauge steel reduced the car's weight by over 150kg and the lightest 'stripped-out' RS cars were below 920kg. The car's coefficient of drag with the ducktail spoiler dropped to CD 0.39. and lift greatly reduced. Competition specification RSs benefited from glass-fibre panels to further reduce weight.

911-930 Turbo series (from 1975) with wide-bodied rear panels. The revised low-drag tea-tray rear wing and the big bumper bellows met new US legislation. The Turbo could touch 160mph and perform 0–60mph in 5.5 seconds. Although wider bodied than a standard 911, it retained the original, 1964 series car's windscreen and side windows. The 911-930 Turbo became the performance car icon of the 1980s. Metallic brown was the colour of the era.

The 1974 Martini-racing liveried 911Carrera Turbo RSR-series with the heavily modified rear wing and front valance (with vented front radiators) to improve downforce and cooling respectively. With 2,142cc and approaching 500bhp and a top speed of 194mph, this car, modified across 1974–6, would take podium places at Le Mans and define a new chapter on Porsche's performance history. The rear wing and body changes were the result of many hours of wind-tunnel experimentation by Porsche.

The 450bhp twin-turbocharged 959 of 1985 used the original 911 centre tub and roof/doors/side windows amid a composite body shell of new front and rear sections. Underneath lay 4x4 and a raft of electronic driver aids. This was a new supercar that took Porsche into the new age of high technology electronic engineering. Three hundred and thirty-seven were built 1985–8. It was derived from the Gruppe B racing car concept study and only external radiator gills significantly delineated between the racer and the production car.

The 993 series morphed into the rather bulbous lines of the Carrera RS and then, as depicted here, the GT2 racer-specification of the 1995–6 era with extended front, side and rear panels. A road-going version was made, but the track version was pure performance. Bolt-on front and rear wing panel extensions made it look bulbous. Underneath, rear-wheel drive and a basic specification created a track and street racer of excellence. 3.6 litres and 430bhp made it rather fast. One hundred and seventy-three were built.

993 series as ultra wide-body GT/RSR developments finally resulted in this GT2-series variant with bolt-on front and rear wing panel extensions which made 993 look bulbous. Underneath, rear-wheel drive and a basic specification created a track and street racer of excellence. The front view shows the deeper front air dam and wider track and body.

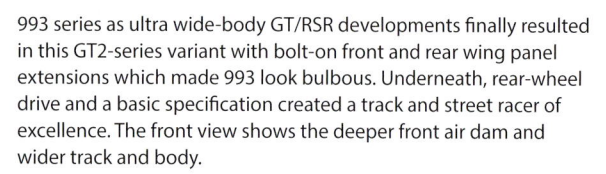

The heavily revised rear spoiler/ wing greatly reduced high speed lift and improved the handling. Under the rear lid was 3.6 litres and 430bhp, which gave it significant speed.

The 911 shape as it evolved is seen here fitted with a GTRS-series rear wing for added downforce. 3.9 litres and the old days of a Mezger engine were replaced with a new Porsche unit. Electric steering and semi-auto PDK became the norm, but a manual GTRS soon debuted. This car was stronger, safer and better-handling than its ancestors. Some say it lost a touch of 911 purism. It is still the essence of Porsche and 911.

This recent, post-2011, 991-series 911 profile shows the classic 911 lineage but a shorter and visually less well-balanced nose section. The redesigned chassis and suspension, with a lengthened wheelbase, reduced rear overhang and improved handling. However, electric steering assistance diluted the 911's purity according to experts. This 180mph+ car still leads the sports car market and was available with 3.4-, 3.6-, 3.8- and 3.9-litre powerplants.

AMALGAM COLLECTION (BRISTOL, UK)
PORSCHE 911
1/18 SCALE

Currently available and arguably one of the world's most exquisitely detailed 911 models in terms of design, detail and production standards is the Amalgam Collection and their renditions of three 911s – from early car to a 2016 variant. These models, produced at 1/18 scale (resin/cast), represent thousands of hours of forensic research, manufacturer liaison and a clever blend of moulded construction. They are of course not aimed at the economy end of the market and are designed to appeal to the dedicated 911 enthusiast. In terms of accuracy, Amalgam's 911 range is so close to full-scale production reality that no amount of praise can do justice to seeing them up close. It is the detailing and scaling of small items that make these kits. Only the wheels and tyres reveal the moulded nature of the rendition. Panel gaps and design motif detailing is excellent. Currently the three Amalgam 911s retail for under £1,000 each and represent the 1/18 scale as opposed to some of the company's more expensive 1/8 scale offerings: a 1967 911R Monza, a 1973 911 RSR/Brumos Racing 2.8 litre, and a slightly less classic 2016 911 GTRS-type derivative RSR as driven by N. Tandy and P. Pilet. The RSR depicts the car of Hurley Haywood who won the Daytona 24 Hours five times and stems from research with Porsche – the original car having been 'lost'. Amalgam also produce a 1/8 scale Porsche 356A in the four-figure market at £8,000.

The Amalgam Collection's 1967 911R Monza edition accurately renders Porsche's 911 story. The R was Porsche's new weapon for sports car racing – the 210+bhp R variant. At Monza over three days in October 1967 this car, chassis #006, drove 1,000 miles (1,609 kilometres) at an average speed of 140mph, 5,000 miles (8,047 kilometres) at an average speed of 132mph and 10,000 miles (16,090 kilometres) at an average of 131mph in a series of record-breaking endurance tests. Amalgam's car is expertly detailed via factory drawings. The R, and this ultra-lightweight R, were the height of early 911 performance specification – the 911 TR being its predecessor. 911 R was the first of the modern era hot-rod road racers. 1/18 scale in expertly cast resin throws off the die-cast metal tradition and takes modelling into a new thinking that some have yet to adapt to. For the accuracy and the price, a new era opens for the enthusiast.

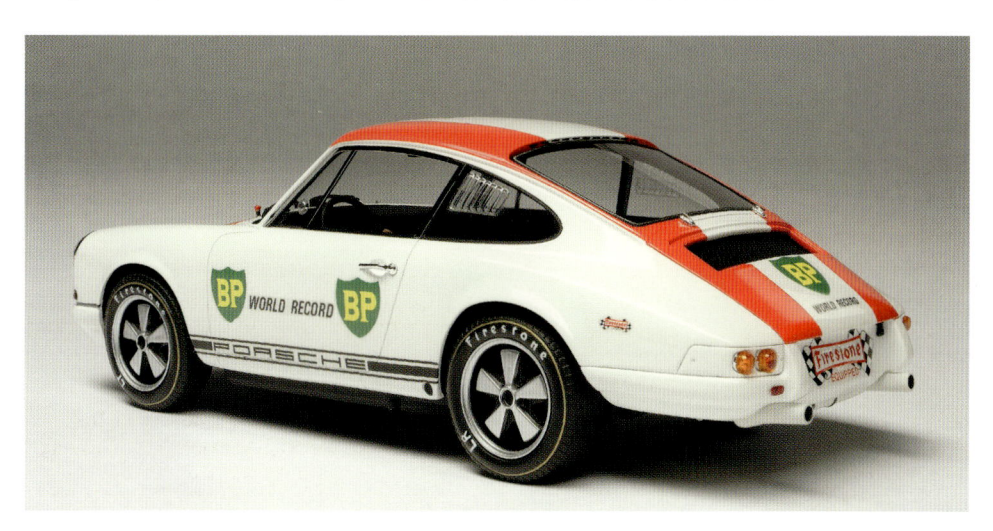

Seen from the crucial rear-side angle, the correct scaling of the 911 has been achieved in the Amalgam 911R. Note the perfect rendition of the rear roof-lip and vents and the vented perspex rear side window: vital details for the modeller. The 7J rear wheels (as opposed to 6J) were unique to the car and had high magnesium content. Their larger size creates the fuller appearance to the wheel-tyre combination.

42 PORSCHE 911: CLASSIC GERMAN SPORTS CAR

The headlamps on this R are also different – using transparent glass and Cibie Bi-iode units. The front horn vent apertures are also non-standard. It is believed that the front indicators were taken from a NSU part. Note the rubber (not leather) straps on the bonnet and rear lids.

With non-standard rear lamps and glass-fibre front and rear lid panels, bumper valances and doors, this unique 911R added lightness.

Model Showcase 43

Seen from above, the 911's carefully tapered hull and roof turret blend together in the ultimate fastback form. The mesh grille over the engine vent is of note to modellers.

The essential ellipsoid profile and Fuchs alloys. You cannot get more 911 than this.

Cockpit detailing of this 1/18 scale model is superb. All the R-type details are correct amid the specification for the Monza 911. The unique oil-filler cap location resulted from Porsche engineers moving the oil tank for better weight distribution.

44 PORSCHE 911: CLASSIC GERMAN SPORTS CAR

Getting the rear roof vents correctly scaled and rendered is not easy but has been expertly achieved here by Amalgam. Also seen is the perspex, vented, lightweight rear side window as used across many racing specification 911s and on recent non-factory special and tribute cars.

Fuchs alloys are the essential detail of classic 911s and many models of the 911. These wheels were fitted to the 911 from the 1970 model year announcement on the 911.2.2-litre T-series. In modelling terms, achieving the correct spoke blade scale and the rim size is key.

In this detail shot we also see accurately rendered the non-standard lights and front valance air vents on this model of the Monza 911. Also on show are the very carefully modelled bonnet-retaining straps and the wheel and tyre combination. This car as modelled, reflects the extensive use of glass fibre in the actual full-scale car itself – notably for the bonnet and the bumper valances.

TAMIYA
911 924 RSR TURBO
1/12 SCALE

Ranging from 1/10, 1/12 1/24 and 1/28 scales, the commitment of Tamiya to the 911 as a model is significant. Tamiya produced the 911 as a kit as early as 1976 as an RSR Turbo Type 934. There soon followed four specific 911 race kits, notably the special-bodied Martin Porsche 935 Turbo with its aircraft-type biplane rear wing. The famous orange *Jagermesiter*-liveried Tamiya 911 Turbo RSR was, and remains, a model for the true Porsche fanatic. Tamiya also produced standard 911 small and big bumper versions of the 1970s 911 body shell. Across various re-boxings, re-toolings and licensings, Tamiya's 911s have demonstrated excellent moulding, detail and design accuracy. Currently, vintage Tamiya 1970s' Porsche kits in good condition fetch three-figure sums on the market. Tamiya's Porsche 959 Sports Car 1/24 scale is now a rare kit indeed. Paul Chenard, the Canadian designer and automotive artist, produced one of the most exquisite builds of a Tamiya 911 934 RSR Turbo (the orange *Jagermeister* model) at 1/12 scale. This model, which took over 350 hours to build, has won numerous awards and is a stunning tribute to the art of model making. Paul has worked wonders on the engine bay and interior. Tamiya's 1/24 Porsche 911 GT2 (Tamiya 24175) comes in several versions including road-going and race-specification. Tamiya also produces electric radio-controlled 911 GTs to 1/10 scale based on the Tamiya TT-02 chassis platform – the successor to the TT-01 with new features.

Here is the actual 'big scale' model itself from Tamiya. It is a wonderfully accurate rendition of a famous 911 and deserves its place among the legend of the 911 and of Tamiya. The modeller can spend many hours working to achieve forensic detailing and finishes on the basis of this famous Tamiya kit.

Paul Chenard says of his model, 'I did extensive research into the engine, hoses, wiring and interior details to get it right; that includes the scale of those hoses and wiring. I even added weight throughout the car so that it would sit correctly.'

Paul Chenard's model of the superb Tamiya #12020 934 RSR Turbo of 2005 (soon to be re-released by Tamiya). The renowned Canadian automotive artist Paul Chenard was, like many, taken with the orange 911 934 RSR series car and spent many hundreds of hours (350 hours plus) building and honing this 1/12 model of the car. It has won several modelling awards and truly depicts the high art of automotive modelling.

'The kit is so detailed that the only extra parts that I had to scratch-make were the headlight bulbs/sockets, an electronic item on the top-right of the alternator, the shift linkage and the front tow hook. A tradition I started with my early race car kits was to honour my dad's memory by adding a ruby from one of his old watches that he gave me to take apart when I was a kid. I like to hide them in plain sight. On the 934 it's on the bottom far left of the dashboard,' observes Paul.

Paul's exquisite detailing included building actual screws into the battery terminal clamps and perfectly replicating the four-point seat harness.

Paul got hold of the Tamiya race team figures and created a diorama to pay tribute to the car and its crew. A great deal of work went into painting and accurately rendering the mechanic's overalls and the logos. For example, the Dunlop patch is a trimmed laser print which Paul varnished and then glued into place. The new Tamiya release of the kit features photo-etched parts. As can be seen, this is the high art of scale model building and of Porsche 911 affection. Paul, and Tamiya have every reason to agree.

48 PORSCHE 911: CLASSIC GERMAN SPORTS CAR

Dashboard delight: Paul Chenard has gone to the forensic level to model the classic 911 five-dial instrument panel and steering wheel detailing. The vinyl treatment to the dashboard is very realistic. Note also the accurately-scaled roll bar section.

The production big bumper specification bellows and the wheel arch extensions allied to the larger alloy wheels are expertly modelled here. This is the standard to aim for.

Below left: Common across racing and road-going high-performance 911s was the revised front bumper design which aided the aerodynamics and incorporated the oil cooler vents. Again, we see what results are possible when you put 350 hours into a model.

Below right: Most competition-specification 911s featured fuel/engine/electrical cut-off handles that were externally mounted for quick access by marshals and rescuers in case of accident. These details can be seen on this superb model where everything has been thought about by its creator.

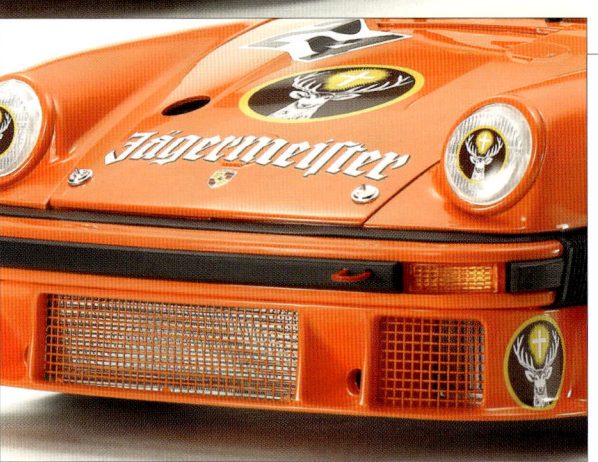

AMALGAM COLLECTION
DAYTONA 24 HOURS 911 RSR #59
1/18 SCALE

By 1973 the 2.7-litre RS and R series 911s had created a cocktail of road and racing specifications. Of note, the RSR was a 2.8 litre of 308bhp (then a 3.0-litre variant) and featured many racing specification upgrades and updates, including revised aerodynamics and spoilers, the addition of a new vent in the front valance to assist the oil cooler, differing wheel rim/tyre sizes front rear, and lightweight glass-fibre body panels to further reduce weight to around 950kg (latterly 920kg). The RSR was big success, not least in America with the Brumos Racing Team of Jacksonville Florida, through which the Porsche name dominated the American racing schedule for several years. The RSR won at Daytona, Sebring and in the Mexico 1000 race. Car #59 was Peter Gregg of Brumos' chosen car and number. Today a new special-edition, full-size 911 GTS liveried in Brumos colours is on sale as a tribute to Hurely Haywood, perhaps the original car's most famous pilot. Featured here is the Amalgam Collection's RSR Daytona #59 model of the 1973 car, of which 200 special edition models, signed by Hurely Haywood, are on sale. The 1/18 scale model is cast in resin, has metal parts and includes the corect manufacturer's paint codes. Car #59 took the Daytona win five times from 1973, yet was lost years later in an acident. Expertly and accurately modelled, this model is a true tribute to the 911 RSR and its legendary racing years.

Adding to the Amalgam Collection's 1/18 scaled 911 output is this superb 1973 911 2.8-litre RSR / Brumos Racing 2.8-litre variant (3.0-litre engined for the 1975 Daytona win). Accurate to the nose-down pitch resulting from the wheel/tyre suspension set up, this is the Hurely Haywood/ Peter Gregg car of Daytona 24 Hours fame complete with ducktail rear spoiler. Hidden is the Norbert Singer engineering contribution to the 'real' car.

Also accurately shown are the windscreen retainer clips, emergency cut-off switches, twin filler caps in the bonnet and revised lighting.

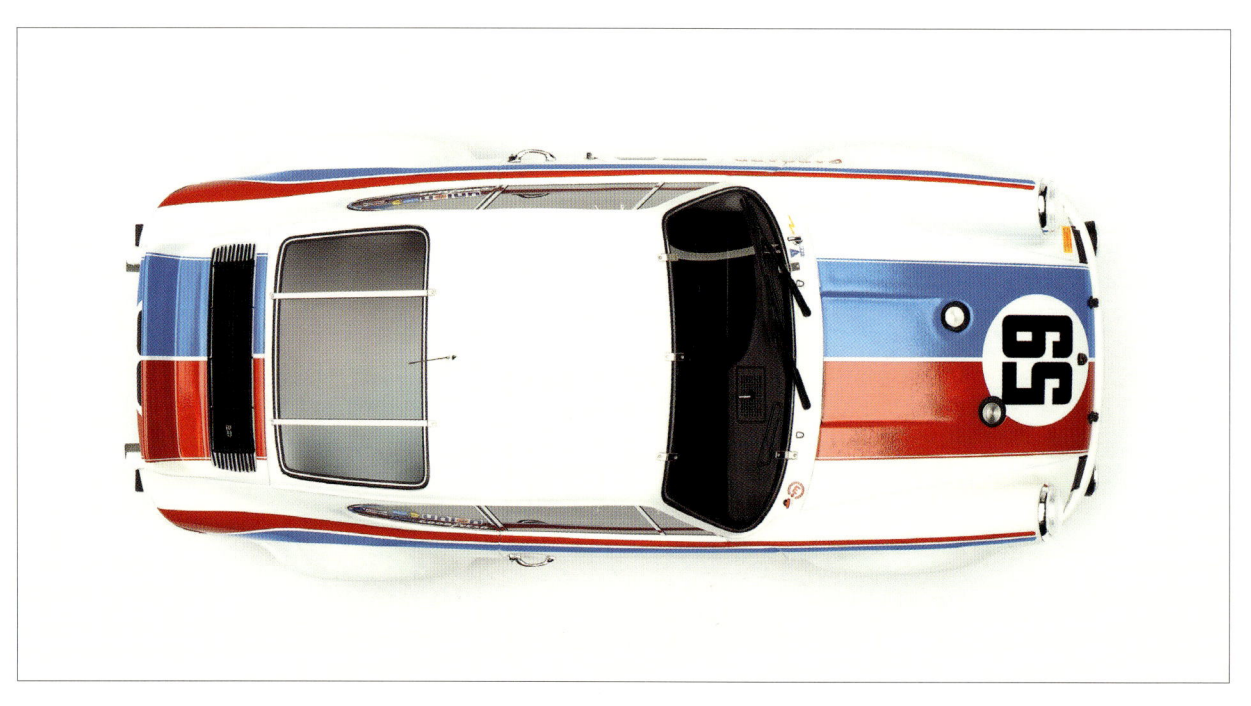

Evident here is the narrow-bodied sleekness of the pre-930 Turbo wide-bodied era. The striping is rather smart too. In 2019, Porsche announced a new RSR series that aped this original specification in looks but took the concept into new technology.

Model Showcase 51

Extra fuel/oil fillers, revised glass-fibre front valance with oil cooler vents, extra lamps and bonnet retaining straps all add exquisite detail in Amalgam's 1973 911 racer rendition.

This car features the essential and defining ducktail rear spoiler as first seen on the 911 RS production series in the early 1970s. The high lip, vertical rear panel, side fences and scooped-out frontal panel adjacent to the engine vent, all work together to reduce aerodynamic lift by over 70 percent and aid engine/cooling venting. Note also the wonderful exhaust system detailing.

Side panel view shows how close Amalgam have got with this 911. The larger rear-wheel size, quick-access jacking point and front windscreen retaining strips are all perfectly scaled and cast.

Model Showcase 53

SCHUCO
PORSCHE 911-991-SERIES TARGA
1/18 SCALE

Seen here is the recent Schuco 1/18 scale die-cast Porsche 911-991-series Targa in the correct and accurately sprayed Porsche iridescent Sapphire Blue, with black trim and black alloy wheels – factory specification for the full-size car and for this model. Schuco of Germany have been making models for many decades and have made great strides in design detail at 1/18 scale and offer very accurate renditions, scaling, colours and materials. Of particular note are the cabin, lamps, wheel and brake detailing. The difficult-to-model Targa roof and rear windscreen have been achieved with exemplary quality. This model was purchased at the Porsche Museum in Stuttgart where many models are on sale. Captured here is contemporary Porsche design at its best.

The current styling of the 991/2-series truly captures the essence of the 911. A return to a Targa-type design with brushed steel B-post roll-hoop took 911 back to the first Targa of the late 1960s. Schuco's 1/18 scale Targa has superb detailing – as seen here in this classic front-quarter view of a great model that the Porsche modeller cannot ignore.

The classic new-age 911 shape is wider and larger than the old 911 classics, yet conveys the historical lineage of the 'Butzi' Porsche styling. The Targa's rear windscreen and rear-deck design is a fine update of the 1960s Targa design motif. That curved rear screen is tough to produce at full scale, yet Schuco have managed it at 1/18 scale. The door handles are also well-integrated.

The sheer level of detail in this model makes it an enthusiast's choice. Note the scale of the headlamps, panels, panel gaps, wheel casting and glass. This is very close to the real thing.

Sheer detail – spoked alloys, drilled brake discs and accurately painted brake calipers – again a perfect match to the full-scale car and tribute to Schuco's work on this superb model.

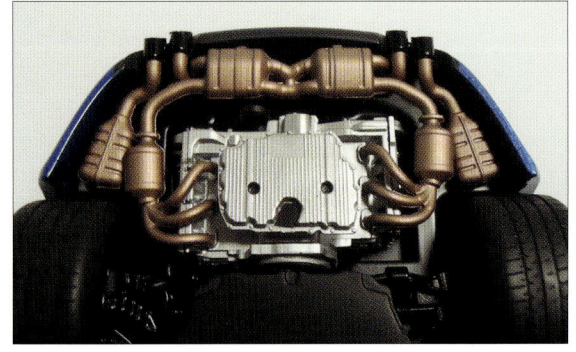

Above: Targa legend depicted in the brushed alloy B-pillar roll hoops and with the vents detailed. The hard-backed sports-seat option has also been modelled as has the seat material. The door-handle detail is also well defined and scaled.

Right: Under the rear end, Schuco provides a good basic level of engine detailing – for the flat-six Boxer-type engine and exhausts. Modification by a modeller's hand can always be added.

Model Showcase 55

The face of the 911 – classic headlamps set amid modern aerodynamic body design and the Porsche signature air vents and lamps. All perfectly scaled – down to the Porsche badge.

The intricate design of the Targa's folding roof, sealing and stow-away Targa roof section which folds downward and inward is a tough feature to model. Note the well-scaled engine vent and badging.

56 PORSCHE 911: CLASSIC GERMAN SPORTS CAR

Speed-sensitive rear spoiler seen deployed at the rear. This reduces aerodynamic lift at higher speeds. On this model it can be closed or open in the activated position – again, accurately scaled as is the Porsche 911 script across the rear valance.

Below: Seen from above the width of the current 911 bodyshell compared to earlier 911s is obvious. Note the Targa details, such as the roll-hoop and open interior.

911 – Stuttgart Style in Scale

Like the full-size car, the modelling of the 911 has proved an enduring feature of the scale model landscape. In die cast, white metal, injected resin/plastic, composite hybrid, and even in wood, the 911 has been modelled across most of its incarnations across a number of scales including 1/10, 1/18, 1/24, 1/28, 1/43 and on occasion in other scales. The car is also a firm favourite with the radio-controlled 1/10 scale, powered-model fraternity, and of course we look to Tamiya's products as the exemplars of moulding and decal accuracy in the enthusiasts' mass-market sector.

From early 901 series through the 'classic' and 'RS' 911 years of the 1970s and early 1980s, to today's GTRS cars, the lifespan of 911 is well documented in modelling history. The car has a global following among model makers.

The various specifications, trims, spoilers, finishes and colour schemes across the 'factory' production cars are well represented. Of note, the various 911 Targa types have also been manufactured as kits – providing interest for those 911 enthusiasts less focused on racing and rally-car specification 911.

However, what is particularly interesting for the modeller is the range of racing and rallying specification variants of the 911 produced by the model-making companies. A great array of liveries, named drivers and specifications has been released across various 911 body styles.

From Le Mans, to Macau, from the Nürburgring to Sebring, the modeller can build highly accurate renditions of very specific 'competition' series 911s and create their own collection of 'race-specification' 911s. Tamiya and of note, Fujimi, now produce a large range of 911 model options across a broad offering of racing types, drivers and liveries.

Modellers are well supplied with 911 decal and accessory options. From liveries, spoilers, wide-body panels, glazing, interiors and highly detailed engine construction options, 911 is a forensic modeller's and modifier's paradise. From the early kits of the 1970s, through the release of several kits in the 1980s, across various licensing and re-box and re-tooling into the 1990s and beyond, all variations of the 911 are now catered for.

Without presenting an advertising resume for model manufacturers, it is important to review the 911 kits that are available and observe just how well served this iconic car has become amid the model moulding and casting manufacturers and their releases.

We must cite Tamiya as devoted 911 model-kit providers, and note Italeri, Revell and the long-established Schuco of Germany and Auto Art as die-cast providers. Across the built and kit-build landscape there are many Porsche manufacturers.

Names such as Advent, Arena Modelli, Automodelli Studio, Hobby Design, Ixo Models, Micro Ace, Maxichamps/Minichamps, Solido and Spark are famous suppliers recorded across 911 model manufacturing. DeAgostini has also produced 911 models in their part-work build series. Other kits in the 911's moulding history include those in the 1990s from Doyusha, Entex Industries, Model Factory Hiro, and more recently, Otaki. Profil 24 also make a 1/24 scale modern 911 race-specification resin model. Autoart offers a rare Porsche 959 white die cast model car at 1/18 scale – amid a range of 911s.

Tamiya is the brand we look to for the ultimate in plastic/resin kit model construction kits. Tamiya's

Tamiya's box art and imagery is well known – as are the company's variously scaled 911-series models. A vast range of liveries and specifications are part of the Tamiya 911 modelling story – as is superb accuracy of moulding and details.

detailing and accuracy even at smaller scale, is very good and when seen beside other offerings, shows where the brand has concentrated on fine and accurate detail moulding, scaling, and the technology to create it. Tamiya's 911 930 Turbo and its 911 993 GT at 1/24 scale, really do remain the benchmarks for the modeller. The now re-issued 'Big Scale' 1/13 provides the modeller with a great basis to work from. Yes, you can add many hours to creating your ultimate kit, but Tamiya's 911 range provides a great start for even the most experienced modeller.

Tamiya 911 1/25 Build notes

Porsche 911 993-series GT2 Club Sport Road Version at 1/24 scale Tamiya (244247/2500)

I approached this kit knowing it was a relatively easy build of a tooling that has been around since the late 1990s. As with all Tamiya kits, you can be assured that the moulding, shape, scaling and details are pretty much spot on and not likely to offend the expert observer's eye.

There were no obvious significant dimple or extrusion issues with the moulding, although a tiny amount of clean-up once some parts came off the sprue was an occasional diversion. But Tamiya's moulding is still a quality job.

Despite the small size of the model at this scale, the window/roof pillars were noteworthy for their correctness. The 'bolt-on' wing/fender extensions were very accurate and their bolt location channels accurately sized and moulded. The roll-cage, interior, wheels and tyres were also all very well scaled and detailed – typical Tamiya attention to design and tooling quality that can only benefit the finished model.

Very little sanding or filling is required – except perhaps around the rear wing 'spoiler' (suggest fitting mesh to the side-plane intakes). Wheel, hubs, tyres, suspension all impressed, as did the accuracy of the front filler panel on the bonnet/hood.

This was the road-going version of the 993 GT2, but having built the racing version, I know it comes with some excellent livery decals. The only real issue with the road-going variant was what Porsche colour to choose? Guards Red, Riveria Blue or GP White? Not silver – surely? And why stick with Tamiya's own paint recommendations? Others exist, notably some closer matches for things like brake pipes and engine components. Applying Tamiya primer, and the acrylic spraying produces a good body finish, but working on the bolt-on wheel arch extension panels' mounting bolts needed a magnifying glass! If you choose to paint

Tamiya's 1993-series 911 GT2 shows off the curves and angles of the car's uniquely extended body. The fine detailing of the window surrounds and roof pillars mean that no, or very little, 'improvement' work is needed by the modeller.

– can you adapt it to a race-specification car and go with a bare metal finish? Alternatively, what about a flat black?

Trying to 'rough up' the tyres is not easy on these tough-finish mouldings and creating an accurate interior rendering requires quite a lot of work. Fitting the windows requires patience! The lamp lenses were superbly rendered and accurately scaled.

Overall, I put getting on for over twenty-four hours into building this kit. The scale at 1:24 means that for a lot of effort, the resulting kit is on the small side, but you know that when you purchase it.

The 993-series had new front and rear wings, and the GT2 variant added further extensions and wheel arch panels. Tamiya have faithfully captured these in their superb scaling.

What cannot be denied is that for the money, and providing the modeller has the skills and patience to work through the Tamiya build process and to step outside the rules, the resulting model is less 'kit' and more scale model of the real thing.

For the price, this is a top quality bargain. It may have been around a long time, but you simply cannot argue with the offering. The only thing to do to really present this kit to its true effect is to create an appropriate diorama – oh and to build the racing-specification model – or models. Time to make and fit the car Riveria Blue, remember that if you use Tamiya TS23 Light Blue, it is not as vibrant and needs self-blending to 'sample to match' as they say at Porsche.

At build, I took a long time laying everything out and pre-preparing and pre-painting much of the interior and under-car fittings before assembling into place. Avoiding the dreaded 'orange-peel' effect is not easy even for an experienced sprayer. Yet this can be polished down when properly dry.

Placing the interior, engine and underframe into the body are the trickier bits of this Tamiya process and strict adherence to the instruction manual is recommended for all but the practised builder.

There is precise work required on painting and fitting the suspension components as well as the interior. The Porsche factory offered several options for the colour of the roll-cage on the road-going version and my choice would be to match the body colour.

Along with other modellers, I choose to remove the chrome plating effect on the wheels and to re-spray them in a softer, more alloyed finish. The interior floorpan presented some thinking in terms of finish

Typical Tamiya: The BBS-Type alloy wheel as 'chromed'. Rendition in a less-shiny, used alloy paint finish is recommended by modellers.

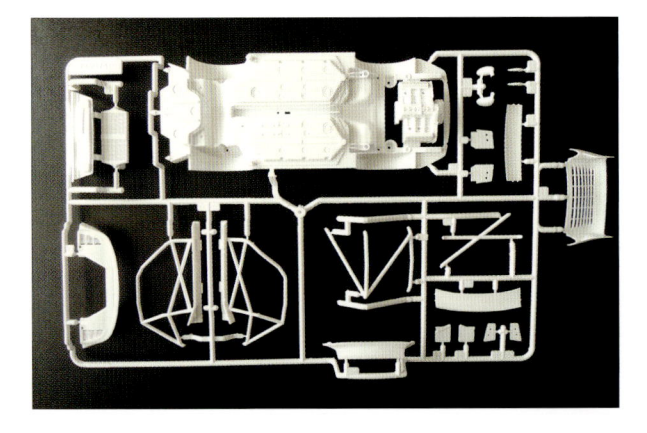

Typical Tamiya mouldings on the sprue. Some minor work may be needed to trim and fettle some of the parts upon detaching them.

some 'dive-plane' aerodynamic devices on the front corners then?

The long-established **Revell** kit, notably that of the 991 930 Turbo, delivers an accessible kit to modellers of all ages. This kit has been around a long time and remains a route into Porsche modelling. Revell released its first 911 kit in 1970 and has a notable history of 911 releases. From 1970 there followed the 911 Carrera Cabrio (Revell 07356); 911 Turbo (Revell 07300); Carrera Cabrio (Revell 67356); Carrera Cabrio (Revell 07063). A later 911 of Revell/Kikoler at 1:25 scale latterly appeared. The Revell 930-series wide-body Turbo kit (07179/still available).

Revell's kit requires a great deal of work to even begin to look as good as it does in the kit's marketing photographs. Details such as roof-pillars, window frames, wheel spokes, and many fittings, all require significant attention to fine-tune their forms as these are thicker in gauge than in the actual production car and are difficult to refine beyond their moulded scaling. Chromework on wheels, and on engine components is basic and requires notable toning down. Despite such criticisms, the general shape of the 911 is accurate. Just be prepared to do a lot of work to approach an expert-grade finish.

Revell have been making 911 kits since the 1970s and however corny this 930 Turbo box art, the true 911 passion is evident. Revell's kits have provided access for the enthusiast and for the dedicated modeller alike. However, this kit's scaling of styling and design details is not as accurate nor as fine-scaled as Tamiya's.

The wide bodied rear wings, 'tea tray' spoiler, and larger wheels of the Turbo-bodied cars is obvious. From 1975 to 1989, the Turbo 930s series defined the Porsche look.

This is the quintessential 911 930-series Turbo 'big bumper rendition by Revell. Only the thickness of the window/roof pillars and the glazing detract from the quality of the kit.

PORSCHE 911: CLASSIC GERMAN SPORTS CAR

Left: Revell body (above) and Tamiya body (below) show detail differences and the superiority of the Tamiya moulding standards.

Below left: Turbo's engine bay was packed with cooling, fuelling and forced induction paraphernalia. Difficult to model accurately.

Below bottom: The interior of Revell's Porsche 911 Turbo.

Key 911 modelling essentials checklist
Engine.
Hoses.
Clips.
Exhaust details.
Wiring.
Roll cages.
Vents.
Shut lines.
Front horn vent moulding.
Bumpers and over-riders.
Window trim – black or metal.
Rear boot/deck spoiler types.
Fuchs wheels or alternatives.
Tyres.
Interior trims.
Seats.
Steering wheel type.
Carpets.
Dashboard and dials.
Fuel and oil filler cap details.
Headlamp and turn lamp specifications USA/ Europe.
Sill trim plates is applicable.
Bumper trims.
Correct model year chrome strips and inserts.
Correct model year badging.
Undertray
Door mirror model-year appropriate.
RS, R, RSR, and Lightweight body alterations and detailing.
Photo etching details. Chrome foil.
Decals (911-series decals are available from many sources including: Renaissance, Studio 27, and Indy Cals).

Modelling the Porsche 911 61

The **Amalgam Collection** tops off the current resin/metal hybrid cast model offering for the 911and brings it to recent times with the 911 GTRS racer seen below.

Below: Porsche vetted Amalgam's model before approving its accuracy. The aerodynamic devices are perfectly rendered.

Amalgam's 2016, 911 GTRS-type derivative of the 991-series 911 racer reflected the recent Porsche racing series. Nick Tandy and Patrick Pilet achieved much fame in this endurance series with the 510bhp, 4.0-litre 911 with its unusual 'rotated' mid-engined configuration – ahead of the rear axle as opposed to trailing it.

Seen from above, the 2016 911 shape differs little from the 1964 and 1970s 911 shapes.

Auto Art is a long-established major player in the die-cast scene and has also moved into hybrid composite casting. Its Signature Collection models, notably the 1/18 scale replicas are finely detailed and the company produces over a dozen Porsche 911 types – and many other Porsche models from across Porsche's history. Auto Art's renditions of classic 1964-8 911s, the 1970s RS cars, and later 911 series including race-specification 911s, all offer superb detailing of the important Porsche design language.

Auto Art also produce a recent 991-series GT-sepc 911 which has sold well.

Of note, a Matrix-manufactured 1/6 scale 911 has recently been announced – another entry into the three-figure cost market. Chinese manufacturer Welly has produced a range of die-cast 911 models including a 1/34 scale 959. Herpa produce die-cast 911s to 1/87 small scale.

Germany's **CMC** also produce a superb range of 911s including a 901-series car of 1964 type. CMC's

The large scale of the Schuco model means better details as can be seen in the body and cabin of this Sapphire Blue 991 Targa. The roll-hoop is well shown as are the body contours and scaling that Schuco expertly have captured.

Schuco have been making models for over 100 years and the 911 is a Schuco favourite. Their excellent 1970s 911 Targa displays superb body, engine, bay and cabin detailing right down to the correct period seat rim and steering wheel

models retail for three figures, they lie above the two-figure prices for mainstream kits and just below the most expensive offerings and are very highly regarded.

Porsche itself offers a wonderful range of fully built, resin-moulded models of all their cars including the very latest model ranges. These models are for sale in official Porsche dealerships. The Porsche 911 Targa 'Rijkspolitie' at 1/43 with the perspex, soft rear Targa section is of note.

Fujimi, founded in 1948 and originally producing wooden models, have been prolific releasers of 1/24 scale 911 variants from 1985. The new 1985 tooling from Fujimi was the 911 Carrera 1973 (08206). Fujimi produced a very accurate 964-series 911 in 1990. In 1989 Fujimi produced a 911 Speedster of note. A noted Fujimi 911 was the early Carrera RSR 'Martini', while as recently as 2013 Fujimi released a 911 Carrera RS 'Hayase Sakon' 1/24 (170053 CW-3). The company also released the 'Kuhne & Nagel' sponsored 911 Carrera rally car at 1/24 (08008/08229).

Schuco, the German model manufacturer that has been in business over 100 years, has also produced a series of excellent 911s. Schuco has made a success of its 911S and 2.4-litre renditions and paid particular attention to the detailing of the flat-six engine – which is superb.

The 1970s' Coupé and Targa are well detailed in the Schuco 'Edition 18' kits at 1/18 scaled die-cast series and they feature opening parts. Curiously these cars have the earlier, external oil filler panel that did not feature on 1973 model year cars. Well shaped, and very 'Porsche' in their feel, these two recent models do however, show some somewhat overdone chrome work and detailing in terms of shapes and scaling. All other details are well rendered, but the the undertray appears to have 'plastic' feel.

Schuco's 'small-bumper' Porsche 911S in metallic gold is, however, a lovely piece of kit and has the true Porsche feel. The shut-lines, window trims, sill-trims, and decals are all excellent.

Italeri have also produced the 911 as a kit across several decades. Key examples of the Italeri and Revell moulding release story respectively include/ 911 Carrera (Italeri 681); 911 Carrera Cabrio (Italeri 679); 911 Turbo (Italeri 682); 911 Carrera Cabrio (Italeri 36790); and 911 Turbo (Italeri 3682).

Spark models have also produced a series of interesting 911s with very well-researched details and features. Produced 'in-house' Spark resin models have a growing reputation for accuracy and build quality. A standard 911, and 'Kremer' 935, RSR, RUF, and modern-era racing 911s are all part of the 1/43 range. A Spark 1/18 range of 911s is also available at higher cost.

A really interesting model is the 1976 Porsche 934 'Vaillant' of Bob Wollek #6 depicted of Team Kremer Racing at 1/12 by **Minichamps**. A Porsche 911 ducktail rear spoiler-equipped car is featured in the **Reji** brand Model SP968 at 1/24.

Other scales and mouldings and castings include/ **Advent** (3103)1/25 911, and the 1/32 1965 Porsche 911S by **Arii** (41023). **Micro Ace** 1/32, (20223) Porsche 911S depicted a 1965 car.

1/43 scale models of 911 include releases by: **AMR** 1/43 911 S Kremer Racing Le Mans´72 #80 Fitzpatrick/Kremer/Bolanos and as 'Toad Hall' Le Mans´72 #41 Keyser/Barth/Garant; **Arena Modelli** released several 911 – 911 MC´67 #219 Elford/Stone; Arena Modelli 911 S 2.4-litre Grp.4 'Porsche Club of America' TF 1972 #23 Barth/Keyser 1/43; 911S 1970 without Decals Fuchs-Style Wheels; **Automodelli Studio** 1/43; **Gamma** releases a1/43 911 RS 'Sonauto BP' Le Mans 1973. (GMK079). In the late 1980s and 1990's, a 1/43 911 Carrera RS (1867 DV 92) and a 'Motul' Le Mans 911SC both came from **Graphyland** of France.

Modern 911. You can walk into a Porsche dealership and buy a 'model' 911. This is the recent 991 series in 'Irish Green' with optional 'chrome' window trim highlights.

Schuco models of the 911 have always been special and this gold 911S 2.4-litre is an excellent rendition of the classic narrow-bodied Porsche 911 styling details. Note use of side decals and black engine vent grille.

64 PORSCHE 911: CLASSIC GERMAN SPORTS CAR

A 1/43 911 Targa from **JPS Miniatures** was just that. Grand Prix models also offer white metal 1/43 scale 911 models and of note offered a Minichamps 'Gitanes'-liveried 911 kit. **Racing 43** branded 911 models from the 1980s also remain on the market. The sheer breadth of the 911 offerings across the marketplace, demonstrate just how popular it was and remains.

Above: Porsche 931 modern day series modelled for Porsche. The original 911 styling cues can be seen lurking under the revised, modern 'aero' package.

Right top: Porsche have just kept on winning at Le Mans and this model of their dedicated Le Mans 919 LMP-series hybrid car is available through Porsche dealers.

Right middle: Porsche's first car and its first model car – the 1950s 356 Speedsteer in all its simple glory.

Right bottom: A very accurate profile of the classic 'small-bumper' 911 that stems directly from the factory material.

Acknowledgements:
The author wishes to acknowledge the following sources for background information:
Communications: Autofarm, Chris Sweeting. The Amalgam Collection. Hobby Co Ltd., Porsche A.G., Porsche GB, Porsche Club GB, Steve Bull Porsche, Tim Read, Dick Lovett (Porsche Centre), Prescott Hill Climb.
Books: *Porsche 911* (PSL Ltd) Paul Frere; *Porsche Engineering for Excellence* (Haynes), Tony Dron; *Porsche, Excellence was Expected* (Automobile Quarterly) Karl Ludvigsen; *The Porsche Book* (PSL Ltd) L. Boschen & J. Barth; *Porsche* (Foulis Ltd) R. von Frankenburg.
Publications: *Autocar, Classic Car, Classic Porsche, Classic & Sports Car, Motor, Porsche Post, Total 911, Christophorus.*

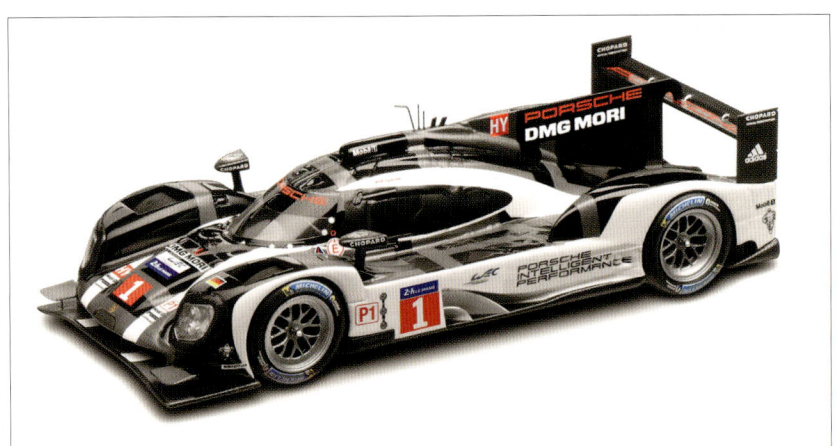

Egg
0-65/70 days

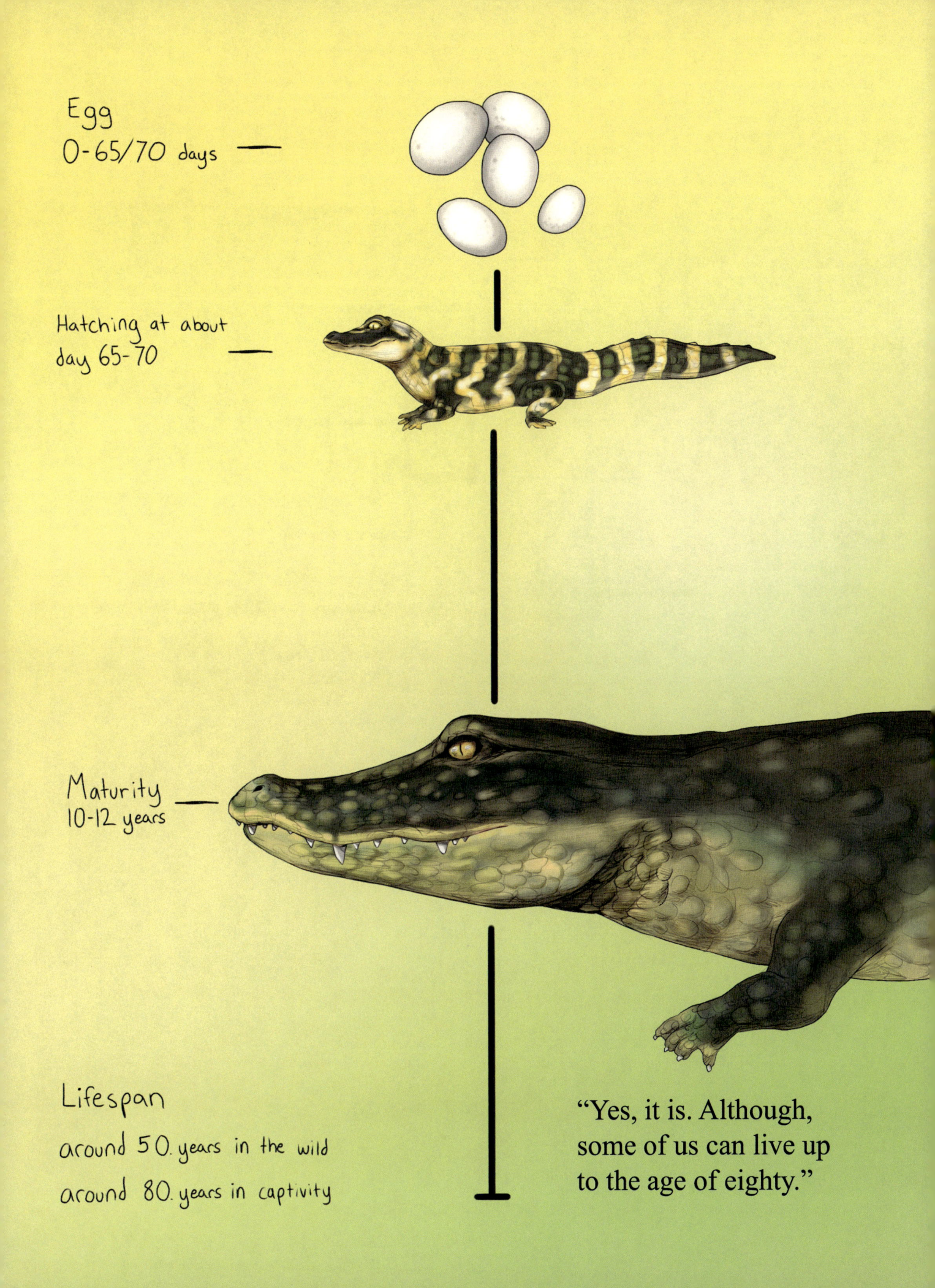

Hatching at about
day 65-70

Maturity
10-12 years

Lifespan
around 50 years in the wild
around 80 years in captivity

"Yes, it is. Although, some of us can live up to the age of eighty."

325 Mya

275 Mya

103 Mya

64 Mya

230 Mya

A common ancestor of two or more species later in time

Mya = Million Years Ago

Mammals

Lizards

American alligator

Gharial (crocodile)

Saltwater crocodile

Dinosaurs that aren't related to birds (ex - T-Rex)

Birds

Evolutionary Rate: Fast — Slow

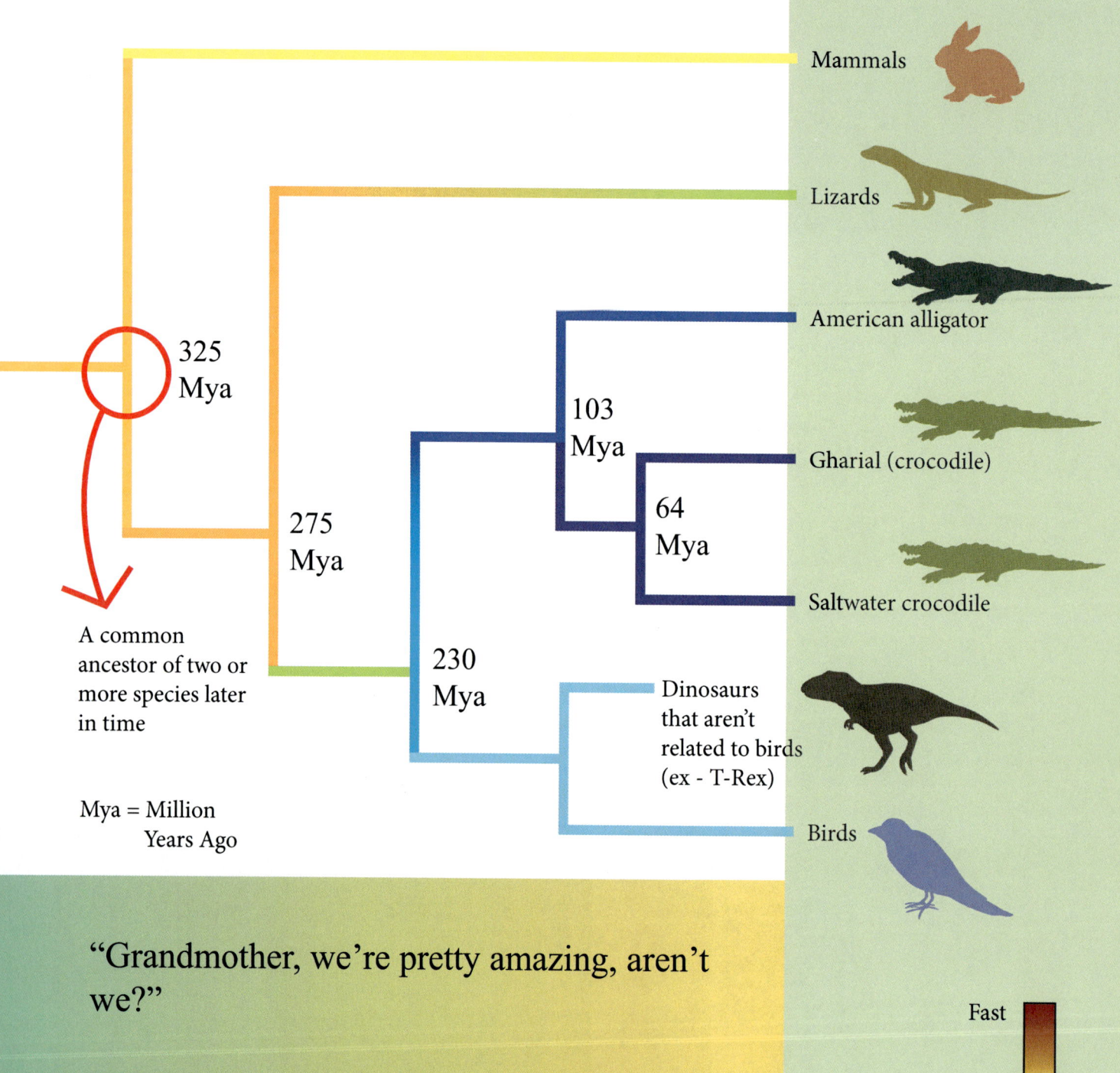

"Grandmother, we're pretty amazing, aren't we?"

"We sure are. And we've got two hundred million years of **evolution** to prove it!"

"What do you mean?"

"I mean that we are older than dinosaurs and that we are all **descendants** from **ancient** families."

"Grandmother, where do we come from?"

"That is a story for another night. Goodnight, my sweet hatchlings."

"Goodnight, grandmother."

Fun Facts

- Alligators come to the wildlife centre that are rescued, surrendered, or injured. They are rescued from skin farms mostly and from people who have exotic pets.

- The alligators stay with the centre until they are approximately 4 feet long. The Florida wildlife commission then ensures that they are sent to a sanctuary after that because they cannot be released or reintroduced into the wild.

- Alligators are a keystone species. The whole ecosystem gets thrown out of whack and everything is connected. These animals were engineered for survival and for evolution. If the Everglades are ever wiped out, it will be an issue for all of humanity.

- Alligators were on the brink of extinction during the 1970's because of hunting, consumption, and fashion. Limits on hunting is helping to slowly restore the population with the introduction of hunting tags.

- There are less than 10 alligator attacks per year in the USA.

- Environmental factors such as loss of habitat due to construction, introduction of invasive species consuming the traditional food sources such as ground nesting birds and small mammals, and humans threaten the conservation of the American Alligator.

- The American alligator is critically endangered in the Miami Keys.

- Alligators can live up to 50 years in the wild and up to 80 years in captivity with proper diet and veterinary care. Health issues that alligators can potentially suffer from are Cayman pox and the common cold.

- Contrary to popular belief, they don't carry salmonella on the outside of their skin, but only in their mouths.

- The only way to tell a male apart from a female is to probe them. Every organ is internal.

- An albino alligator lacks melanin and there are less than 100 in the entire world. They don't last in the wild due to their lack of camouflage, sunburn, and sunstroke.

- We can help with their preservation and conservation by not introducing more invasive species into the wild, stopping breeders and exotic pet owners from releasing then into the wild. Hurricane Andrew levelled a Florida research facility a few years ago and the animals inside were released into the wild that shouldn't be there. International ships emptying their ballast pumps can accidentally release invasive species into the oceans that they don't belong in.

Glossary

Hatchling: A young animal that has recently emerged from its egg

Lurked: Remain hidden to wait for someone or something

Provisions: Providing or supplying something for use

Survival: Continuing to live or exist, typically in spite of an accident, ordeal, or difficult circumstances

Bite Force: Any force exerted upon the occlusal surfaces of teeth. How hard something can bite

Detect: Discover or identify the presence or existence of something

Vertically: Aligned in such a way that the top is directly above the bottom

Evolution: The process by which different kinds of living organisms are thought to have developed and diversified from earlier forms during the history of the earth.

Descendants: Someone or something related to a person or group of people or animal/group of animals who lived at an earlier time

Ancient: Belonging to the very distant past and no longer in existence

The author during her visit to the Alligator and Wildlife Discovery Center, 2021, Madeira Beach, Florida, USA.

The main threat to wildlife around the world is habitat destruction.
Here's how you can help save animals (including alligators!) and the places they live:

· **Pick up litter -** Trash such as paper, cans, bottles, and anything lying in a public place that doesn't belong there is considered litter. Ask an adult to help you pick up litter and properly dispose of/recycle it.

· **Pack a litterless lunch -** Use reusable containers, drinking cups/thermos, and items that can be washed and used again when packing your lunch.

· **Plant only native species of plants and trees -** Native species of plants and trees mean plants and trees that belong in the area and naturally grow in the environment. Planting native plants and trees in the area where you live helps provide natural habitats for surrounding wildlife.

· **Encourage your family to use non-toxic household cleaners -** Toxic cleaning supplies can seep into water reserves and damage the health of wildlife and the environment. Ask your family to use non-toxic cleaners and environmentally friendly products.

· **Recycle -** Recycling is vital for making the environment a cleaner place, conserving materials, saving energy, and reducing the amount of garbage in landfills. Collecting and changing items into something else is recycling. Glass, aluminum, cardboard, and plastic can all be recycled.

· **Use less water -** Take shorter showers, turn off the tap when brushing your teeth, and soap up your hands before turning on the water. These tiny changes can add up to big results and help save water!

Remember, extinction is forever, but together, we can make a difference!